# Kingdom Prophetic
# Lifestyle

# Kingdom Prophetic Lifestyle

*Themes:*
*The King – a Kingdom*
*The Word – a Prophecy*
*The Response – a Lifestyle*

Chris Larkin

**New Wine Press**

New Wine Ministries
PO Box 17
Chichester
West Sussex
United Kingdom
PO19 2AW

ISBN 978-1-905991-02-0

Typeset by CRB Associates, Reepham, Norfolk
Cover design by CCD, www.ccdgroup.co.uk
Printed in Malta

## What others are saying about this book...

I was caught off guard by Chris Larkin's book, *Kingdom Prophetic Lifestyle*, because a rare occurrence took place – God changed me as I read it! In this age of information overload, that experience takes you by surprise. It should be no surprise, however, that Chris Larkin is a penetrating writer. Having known her for years. I know that her keen prophetic insights have consistently produced good fruit. As one would expect from someone who hears from the Creator, Chris writes creatively. Her words carry divine, creative power to transform your life. *Kingdom Prophetic Lifestyle* will not only expand your revelation of God and His kingdom, you will also be empowered to see His kingdom come in your own life and the lives of those around you.

**Doug Christoffel** – *Director, Into His Harvest Training School, Regina, Canada*

Chris has faithfully pursued the Lord with a passion to see the prophetic gift be multiplied within the body. To this end she has trained and released many in the gift of prophecy. Her teaching is practical and grounded in Scripture. She carries a strong sense of times and seasons and the final chapter on this subject should be read to gain insight into the times in which we live. Read the book, and allow the Spirit of prophecy to impact your life.

**Martin Scott** – *Sowing Seeds for Revival, Author of* Impacting the City

With the abundance of 'prophetic words' that have been given in church today what a delight it is at long last to have a book that in a simple way explains and deals with the issues of the King and His kingdom and how we handle and interpret such prophecies. This book should have a wide readership it will help many who are on the journey of discovering their destiny in God.

**Norman Barnes** – *Founder of Links International Missions Network*

Our family of churches in the Plumbline Network have benefited greatly from the wisdom, teaching and prophetic insight Chris has brought. With her generous heart to serve, we have experienced first hand her passion for the King and His kingdom. She is one who connects and communicates well with both individuals and congregations. I can recommend her ministry and book knowing it will help build the Lord's house.

*Simon Matthews – Team Leader, Plumbline Ministries International*

What an excellent resource! Not only has Christine Larkin an excellent prophetic ministry, she has also an ability to teach and equip the Body of Christ with excellence. I have had great help in my own ministry from hers. I highly recommend this book. It is refreshing and unlike any other approach to this subject. Christine Larkin has a passion for Jesus and for His Bride. You will feel that through the pages of this book. She is faithful in ministry and as a friend, humble and full of joy and fun. It must have something to do with her Irish root! It was a special pleasure to invite her to minister in Norway, and from the churches where she was invited to teach we got very good reports back to us. We live in radical times. This book is for radical believers in Jesus!

*Bjørn Olav Hansen – Prayer Leader and Founder of Poustinia, Norway*

Chris Larkin represents a new generation of prophetic voices emerging in these opening years of the twenty-first century. In this book, her clear insight provides valuable analysis of the present transitional season of the Western church and explains some of the foundational issues which are at the heart of it. Chris has had many years experience in training and equipping prophetic people, internationally, and draws from these in her writing. *Kingdom Prophetic Lifestyle* will be of significant value to those wishing to understand more of the times we face, and of the uncharted waters which lie ahead of us.

*Peter Stott – Conference speaker and Team Leader, Portsdown Community Church, UK*

Chris Larkin has an ability to show us the ways in which the Lord speaks today so that we say, 'Of course!' but it's only afterwards that we realise that it was her gifting and obedience to the Spirit that made it so obvious. It has been my privilege to hear and to work alongside Christine Larkin, and I readily endorse this book as a distillation of the wisdom and discernment I have already seen and heard in her ministry.

*Derek McKelvey – Minister, Fisherwick Presbyterian Church, Belfast, and Chairman, Kairos Trust*

# Contents

# Foreword

I have known Chris Larkin since around 1989. She was part of many of my early Schools of Prophecy and, with her husband John, moved to Southampton, UK, to be part of the 'team', travelling and running schools of prophecy throughout Europe.

Chris has a great passion for the church. She is a lover of God and the bride to which He is committed. An excellent communicator with a wonderful capacity to empower, equip and release people into their identity, gifting and significance in the Spirit. She has a highly developed and powerful anointing in prophecy.

This book, *Kingdom Prophetic Lifestyle*, is typical of her ministry. Packed with practical insights, wisdom and revelation … it's a serious piece of work and a great development tool for individuals and small groups.

Chris is a pragmatist. Her heart questions are always:

- Does it empower people to be bigger and better?
- Will it work against the enemy?
- Will people discover the Lord in a more powerful way?

She has that specific threefold anointing. Chris, with her husband John, are two of my closest friends. I have watched them grow and prosper in the Spirit when everything has been against them. I love being in team with them.

Their honesty, integrity and faithfulness are proven. They are a living and practising embodiment of their own revelation. They are deeply authentic, powerful people who really, really understand God's heart for His people.

If you can't get them into your church or your region, get the book! Better still . . . get both. You won't be the same again!

*Graham Cooke*
*Author and speaker*

# Introduction: It Started with a Word

> Then God said, 'Let us make man in our image, in our likeness, and let them rule over the fish of the sea and the birds of the air, over the livestock, over all the earth, and over all the creatures that move along the ground.'
>
> So God created man
>   in his own image,
> in the image of God
>   he created him;
> male and female
>   he created them.
>
> God blessed them and said to them, 'Be fruitful and increase in number; fill the earth and subdue it. Rule over the fish of the sea and the birds of the air and over every living creature that moves on the ground.'
>   Then God said, 'I give you every seed-bearing plant on the face of the whole earth and every tree that has fruit with seed in it. They will be yours for food. And to all the beasts of the earth and all the birds of the air and all the creatures that move on the ground – everything that has the breath of life in it – I give every green plant for food.' And it was so.
>   God saw all that he had made, and it was very good.
>
> (Genesis 1:26–31)

All creation started with a word. Have you thought about that? Our Father, Creator, Lord and King spoke a word and everything started God speaks and *life* happens.

Think about it. God, as Father, Son and Holy Spirit, the three persons of God, in communion and communication, had an intention. A glorious intention for what we call Creation and a plan for endless purpose, in and through every created thing.

Life bursting into life, and more life and so on. Endless goodness. Endless fruitfulness.

## The Plan

Man – imaging who God is. Man 'like' God. Made in His 'likeness'. Man – who is not God, but like God. A re-presentation on earth of the person of God; man administering with the delegated authority of God; taking His will in heaven and establishing it on earth.

*God said it was good.*

Have you thought about the supreme importance of that 'word'?

God didn't just have a good idea called Creation. He didn't just 'decide' to make the world. The Trinity didn't just have a conversation and so everything started.

No. It didn't happen at the point when God planned it to happen. Something else was needed before anything could have substance.

It required a speaking forth, a release of a word. Yet in that word was all of God's intention for Creation. That word contained the eternal Plan for everything and everyone that ever was, is or will be.

Words imply meaning and have power. God's word held His meaning and was released with such accompanying power that heavens, earth, planets, plants, creatures and mankind all came into being.

So you and I are here because of a word. God said . . . and there was. Let there be . . . and there was. Until He said it, it did not exist. But when He spoke, life burst into being.

As it was in the beginning, so it is now. God's word is still going out. He is still speaking to His creation today.

God, our God, is a relational God. He relates to the Godhead, three-in-one. There is love, fellowship, preferring, relationship and *communication* at the very heart of who God is.

We are made in His image. Male and female. We are made for love, fellowship, preferring, relationship and communication. Communication with God and with one another. Adam didn't just get Eve for the sake of reproduction – he *had* to have another being who was different, one who he could be in relationship with – just like God is one – yet three; three distinct persons yet one through relationship. Man and woman become one. The Body of Christ is called to be one – even as Jesus and the Father are one. Relationship, communication and unity are all aspects of God and they are God's perfect plan for us.

There's something about these three aspects that reflect the holiness of God. As we embrace these, so we reflect something of the personal holiness of God. That is why Jesus prayed for unity as His last prayer. He knew that without unity anything the disciples did would limit the reflection of God. He knew that when others saw mankind restored to that perfect unity in relationship others would see and believe in Him. For us to love requires another who receives that love. We cannot love alone.

## Who are we – here on earth – in this time and season?

The twenty-first century is rapidly becoming the era where we cease to be contained in our national or local communities. We are now a global people. Communication and culture have changed in only a few decades to a state beyond most people's imaginations. We have instant contact 24-7. We can have a virtual community as our point of relevance and access to limitless information. We can chat with complete strangers across the globe and believe we have relationship. We can wire ourselves up to our MP3 players, keep in constant communication through text and email every hour of every day without actually making physical contact with another human being.

It's an amazing time. It's a dangerous time. It's a time that accommodates separation.

I've just got a wireless laptop computer and I'm fascinated that I can send emails and communicate to people all across the world without being connected to any wires. I can now make videophone contact with friends across the world; we can see each other and hear each other across thousands of miles. How does it work? Words, voices and pictures 'fly through the air' and reach me in my living room – that's normal life in the twenty-first century.

We've also just bought a satellite navigation system for our car and that's even more amazing. A 'human' voice talks to us and guides us through specific roads, correcting us when we go wrong. How does she know?

When I was a child these were the things of fantasy and science fiction. Yet within my lifetime we are seeing wonders beyond belief. Now they are with us we accept them as normal tools of twenty-first-century living.

Yet when we talk about a God who speaks directly into our lives most people would find it incredible. They may rationalise and question why God would want to speak into individual lives; or question the need for a God when we have all the science and technology necessary to meet all our needs – or, if not, we soon will. The pride of life that says, even if there is a God, we can do fine on our own.

## Adam

Adam knew God. He recognised His higher authority and his own role in administering that authority on earth. He was the subject of God, his King.

Having a king implies relationship, authority, rule and reign. It implies others being subjects of that authority.

I wonder what your reaction is to those words. It can feel uncomfortable to those who like to emphasise the freedom we have in Christ. It can imply constraint and restraint on our lives.

But the essence of that truth, which seems paradoxical to human thinking, is that our freedom is only effective in the context of being under the authority of the King, living the kingdom life He planned for us.

So it was with Adam. So it is today.

Abraham heard God, believed Him and lived by faith. His was a prophetic lifestyle.

Moses received a 'prophetic word' and led a whole nation out of slavery into a journey towards the fulfilment of that word.

Joshua held on to that word and took it forward into the land of promise.

Then came the kings, establishing their own kingdoms until one day the King of kings came to earth and the kingdom of God was released to all those who believe and obey.

## The way

*A highway will be there;*
*it will be called the Way of Holiness.* (Isaiah 35:8)

*A voice of one calling:*
*'In the desert prepare*
*the way for the LORD . . .'* (Isaiah 40:3)

*'I will send my messenger, who will prepare the way before me.'* (Malachi 3:1)

*'I am the way, the truth and the life.'* (John 14:6)

The Hebrew meaning of 'way' related to a path, a journey and a way of life. The human life we live on earth is shaped by our birth, culture, experience, interests and human desires. It is how humankind attempts to order time and make sense of life on earth.

However, all our attempts to live a life worth living will fall short of the divine plan unless the Divine Plan rules the life.

The prophetic lifestyle is one that is shaped and directed by that very Divine Plan, revealed and released to our hearts and minds, through the power of the Divine Presence, the Holy Spirit working in and through us. We are to be one with Christ – the Way.

> *If you have ... any fellowship with the Spirit ... then make my joy complete by being like-minded, having the same love, being one in spirit and purpose. Do nothing out of selfish ambition or vain conceit, but in humility consider others better than yourselves. Each of you should look not only to your own interests, but also to the interests of others.*                    (Philippians 2:1–4)

Under the old covenant sacrifices were made in the *entrance* to the Tent of Meeting – not outside. They were known as 'peace offerings' or 'fellowship offerings'. An entrance is a place where people come in – and go out. In the new covenant we know that the Lord has fulfilled all the requirements of the law and the practices. But these sacrifices still reflect His heart's desire that His people are right with Him – and others – before coming into His presence. The Lord's prayer proclaims this – as we forgive others so that the Lord may forgive us. We need to make our way clear of anything that will block or hinder us and this usually means clearing our hearts and minds of things we have against others.

The fruit of a life of fellowship with the Spirit and others will be evident through our humility and our care for others. Where the fruit of a relationship results in condemnation, criticism or control, there is a barrier to fellowship. We must be careful not to allow barriers to be constructed in our way to the Lord. Nor must we create any barriers for others. Christ came to make a way, to bring freedom and a life so full of abundance in Him that joy will permeate our being and the places we inhabit.

This book will look at what it means to live in the kingdom, receive prophetic revelation and live in that revelation. Man living by every word that comes from the mouth of God (see Matthew 4:4).

It's not a fairy tale – it's better than that. All good fairy tales end with the 'happy ever after' and that's the ultimate truth of Christianity. But while we are on earth our purpose is about bringing the kingdom of God into our broken, fallen world. Even when the brokenness of this world impacts our own lives, we can access the One who has a greater Plan for us and receive His specific word of power into our human experience.

## The cross in our lifestyle!

It is impossible to write about the kingdom life without making it clear that all that we do is centred around the truth of the cross. If you read this book without the cross being central to all that is written you will read about human responses and actions. If you read this book with a desire to serve Christ through receiving and releasing His prophetic gift, you will see the power of God change your heart and mind to make the main thing, the main thing – the truth that Christ died, rose and lives to restore the children to their Father. This is the prophetic word we live by.

So as you read on about living a prophetic lifestyle, I pray you will embrace the foundation of life, which underpins all that we are called to be and do – Christ crucified.

# PART 1

## *The Kingdom Story*

# Everyone Is Looking for a King

> *And the L*ORD *told him: 'Listen to all that the people are saying to you; it is not you they have rejected, but they have rejected me as their king.'*            (1 Samuel 8:7)

We are all here because of a word. **The Word** spoke and life happened. In the beginning was the Word ... and the Word was a King.

He came to establish a kingdom – His kingdom – He is the King and we are His subjects. That kingdom is ours and we can live in the goodness of it.

This book is all about that kingdom coming into our lives and us living the kingdom.

The kingdom comes when we hear, respond and release His will on earth.

The prophetic is the mechanism for hearing and releasing. Discipleship is about doing it!

## Who's the King?

There's always a king in our lives. Always was, always is, always will be. An authority outside of ourselves – someone, or something, which has power or influence over our lives.

Who, or what, are kings in our lives? We can have many of them and our challenge is to get the right King on the throne and then allow His kingdom to be established in us and through us. His kingdom is where His will is done – on earth as it is in heaven. Our twenty-first-century life provides a wealth of 'kings' to follow – so many choices, opportunities; so much freedom to choose.

What do you spend most of your time thinking about? It could be an indication of a king in your life. Does that thinking have rule and authority over you? Many years ago I was a high school teacher and I worked with a very grumpy, middle-aged man who taught maths. I noticed that this man was always the last out of the staff room when the bell rang for lessons to start and the first one back in the staff room at break and lunchtimes. He seemed to resent his pupils and never spent time preparing lessons. He had a pile of yellowing, old notes, randomly scattered around his desk and chair, which were his lesson plans. When he reluctantly left his desk to teach he would just pick up any paper and teach on that. This was in the days before the English National Curriculum, when teachers were mainly free to teach without fear of the inspectors calling!

One day I was brave enough to ask this man if he liked teaching, as I was so enthusiastic about my own group of pupils. He looked at me with scorn and told me to wait and see how I felt after thirty years of teaching the little monsters. He said he was just waiting for his pension so he could escape and have a life! I was shocked and amazed that someone could spend thirty years in a job he hated, without any job satisfaction or anything to show for all those years of work. I wonder now what happened to that man. Did he finally get the life he wanted? But what about the thirty years he'd lost in the waiting? The promise of the pension was a 'king' in his life. He thought about it all the time and it enabled him to suffer his teaching job with the hope of a new future. He was happy to pay a huge price of being unfulfilled and miserable just for the possibility of a few retirement years doing what he wanted.

So – even the promise of a pension can be a king, or maybe the king is a job, a person, a home, 'having our own way', having our 'freedom', our culture, nationality – in fact anything that has a hold on our lives, thoughts, emotions, behaviour or choices can be ruling us.

It was for freedom that Christ was revealed – that freedom means we are not to be ruled by anyone or anything other than Christ the King.

Maybe our jobs are ruling us. Of course we need to have resources to live and they are commonly obtained through some kind of work. The issue is not the reality or validity of what is necessary in our lives – rather the issue is the authority they have. Are we controlling them or are they controlling us?

It is the Father's delight to bless us with good things and He does. The test for everything in our lives is the fruit that is produced. A good tree produces good fruit. God looks for the fruit of His blessing as a measure of our stewardship. Are the things in your life a blessing and a joy to you, to others? Do they fulfil their purpose in your life? Material things are useful and a help to enable us to live in the provision and freedom of God. It's not what we have that is the issue; it's the *fruit* of having them that is the issue.

Jesus did not say that money was the root of all evil, but He did say that the love of money was! Money, and what it can buy, can be a great blessing to us and others – but we can't love it as it will rob us of our relationship with God. Jesus was very clear on this. In fact He had more to say about money than anything else! We cannot serve two masters (see Matthew 6:24).

When we serve God we can have a healthy relationship with money.

A friend of ours was a faithful Christian who struggled with having any surplus money. He was happy with just enough provision to pay the bills but was tormented by any excess finances. As soon as he could he would give this money away because he felt guilty having anything more than the minimum amount necessary for living. He hadn't the capacity to live in the abundance and generosity of His Father's blessing. While there was possibly some good resulting from his giving to others, the *fruit* of God's blessing was not evident in this man's life. He was unwittingly despising the generosity of God. It cost him nothing to give the money away – in fact it was a relief. But God's purpose of blessing him personally was completely lost because of his lack of understanding of the Father's love and heart towards him. This man was not serving God with his money; he was turning the fish into stones (see Matthew 7:9)!

While an observer may have thought this man, through his abandoned giving, was exceedingly generous and not at all under the control of money, in fact the opposite was true. Fear of money ruled his life. He feared the responsibility of handling the money and the possibilities of the damage that wrong use of money could do to him. The Lord may have wanted the joy of seeing this son delight in His provision. He may have had a specific plan for that money in the man's life, but the over-ruling objective for this man was to get rid of this money as quickly as possible, often without prayer or thought of God's purposes.

This man was ruled by 'another' king, though his desire and passion was to serve God. The fruit of the blessing was fear, due to his negative response to what was meant to be a blessing from God.

Isn't it interesting how subtly the enemy can work to turn God's blessings into 'kings'? He can then work on establishing these kings and the consequent kingdoms in our lives. Many Christians are confused by the lack of joy and power in their lives, which are really the result of being ruled by another king.

### Adam

Adam had God as his King, he had direct access to the presence of God *and* he had a relationship with Him.

All information and communication was available to Adam from God. He had been given the job of ruling, under God, on earth, establishing and prospering it. It was God's plan to release His delegated authority to a man. He is the true King and our lives are perfected in the divine order of man and woman operating under His kingly authority. We lack nothing. But it wasn't enough to stop Adam wanting more. There was always the question of whether there was more. The ultimate authority for Adam was God's word. That word was full of provision, promise, prosperity and purpose. That word was more than enough for the man – and woman.

But they wanted more – and got it. It was more than they imagined, planned or could handle.

They lost. We lost. The plan was lost.

From that moment on there was a plan within the Plan – a restoration plan.

Our journey in our time on earth is all about getting in line with the Plan. We are restored into the Plan.

Every human being has a deep desire and inner recognition of the Plan. Every human being came from the same origin and place. We were created in the heart and mind of God and spoken forth by the word of God.

So, we try and restore the Plan in our lives. Of course, we don't know that's what we're doing, but our spirits are searching for that perfect place of 'being' and 'doing' which we strive for. We want to know we have value, are significant. We want our lives to have meaning and purpose. Which is exactly what the Plan was all about!

Without God, or occasionally with Him, we make our human efforts to fulfil the Plan. Because of God's delegated authority to mankind we *do* have the power to establish either His will or our will on earth. God never changed His mind and so we should not be amazed at what humans can do. The divine DNA is within us all – for we are made in Him (see John 1).

Every human being has the potential and possibility to do wonderful and amazing things on earth. All creation on earth is subject to humans. But the Fall cut off the union with the Creator Himself. So now, without God, we can still do amazing things, but they are corrupted by fallen nature, usually separate from God. Scientific and technological advances are moving at a shockingly rapid rate – seemingly out of control and certainly out of moral restraint. Who can say what is right or wrong anymore? The development of mankind's ability to create and destroy is un-paralleled. Yet there is a mounting opposition between those who believe science is the ultimate king and those who believe there is a spiritual dimension to life on earth with personal responsibility and consequence.

The original, and everlasting, Plan has God as 'King', integral to it. Man, and all creation, designed to recognise and respond to the ultimate authority, yet living in the freedom of the delegated authority on earth. The divine order.

All fallen-ness is marked by attempts to restore what we have lost. Of course we don't consciously do this, but we strive to fill the emptiness with works of our own power.

## Kings and kingdoms

Jesus came to re-establish the kingdom of God on earth. As it was in the beginning, so it is again.

As we choose Christ as King in our lives we enter the battle-ground of establishing His kingdom in our lives. The flesh nature is used to being king and it doesn't easily give up control. We have our new, true, spirit selves, in which we are established in Christ, led by His Spirit and live in the knowledge of truth. Yet we struggle to dethrone the old nature.

Every day and in every choice or challenge we face, we have to choose whether to follow the Spirit or move in our own choices. Two kingdoms. Two paths. Two outcomes.

Adam's dilemma was that maybe God's way wasn't the best way. Maybe God had not really meant them not to eat. Maybe there was another voice to consider.

That's the problem. We have choice. Adam had choice before he fell. Yet even in his pre-Fall nature he still made the wrong choice. Freedom to choose is freedom to get it wrong.

To have a king is to have an establishment of authority, rule, reign, control, favour and judgement in our lives. In the twenty-first century, there are many dictators and rulers who are 'kings' in their nations. Any human 'king' who is subject to God and desires to serve Him can use his authority and power for good. However, it was never God's plan for man to need a king. God's plan, after the Fall, was to restore communication with His people on earth.

## God speaks to man

Communication is a process by which we transmit information or declare intention towards one another. It requires a sender, a message and a receiver. Successful communication is when the message is received as intended without distortion.

God re-established communication after the Fall by identifying two functional roles on earth to provide two-way communication between Himself and His people. These roles were prophets and priests. Prophets were the ones who received the message from God. They had direct access and communication to Him and were to present His will to the people on earth. In the Old Testament people would consult prophets to find out God's will and they had governmental authority to direct the people.

Priests were to represent the people to God. They were to communicate on behalf of the people back to God.

So there was a planned restoration of the two-way communication and it was sufficient for the time until Jesus came to establish personal relationship and communication through the Holy Spirit's presence among us.

That all changed in the time of Samuel and this, to me, is one of the saddest and most shocking responses of man to God that is recorded in the Bible.

Samuel had been the recognised prophet in the land, he led them into battles and the people listened to what he said.

However, at the end of his days he had not prepared his sons to follow in God's ways and the people were unhappy. The elders, on behalf of the people, had been looking at the other nations around them and saw that they had kings, rather than prophets, to lead and direct them and they coveted these powerful leadership roles. It seemed a better plan than God's plan.

The role of the elders in communities was to ensure the people followed the Lord, obeyed the laws and were cared for. They administered God's authority on earth – as ordained by God to man These elders were aware of their roles and responsibilities and so their decision, as recorded in 1 Samuel 8, is astonishing and indicative of man's fallen response even when there is a direct, explicit word of God about the consequences. It is a lesson to us all and we can reflect on how we choose to respond in our own lives when our wills come in direct conflict with God's.

## Israel asks for a king

*When Samuel grew old, he appointed his sons as judges for Israel. The name of his firstborn was Joel and the name of his second was Abijah, and they served at Beersheba. But his sons did not walk in his ways. They turned aside after dishonest gain and accepted bribes and perverted justice.*

*So all the elders of Israel gathered together and came to Samuel at Ramah. They said to him, 'You are old, and your sons do not walk in your ways; now appoint a king to lead us, such as all the other nations have.'*

*But when they said, 'Give us a king to lead us,' this displeased Samuel; so he prayed to the Lord. And the Lord told him: 'Listen to all that the people are saying to you; it is not you they have rejected, but they have rejected me as their king. As they have done from the day I brought them up out of Egypt until this day, forsaking me and serving other gods, so they are doing to you. Now listen to them; but warn them solemnly and let them know what the king who will reign over them will do.'*

*Samuel told all the words of the LORD to the people who were asking him for a king. He said, 'This is what the king who will reign over you will do: He will take your sons and make them serve with his chariots and horses, and they will run in front of his chariots. Some he will assign to be commanders of thousands and commanders of fifties, and others to plough his ground and reap his harvest, and still others to make weapons of war and equipment for his chariots. He will take your daughters to be perfumers and cooks and bakers. He will take the best of your fields and vineyards and olive groves and give them to his attendants. He will take a tenth of your grain and of your vintage and give it to his officials and attendants. Your menservants and maidservants and the best of your cattle and donkeys he will take for his own use. He will take a tenth of your flocks, and you yourselves will become his slaves. When that day comes, you will cry out for relief from the king you have chosen, and the LORD will not answer you in that day.'*

*But the people refused to listen to Samuel. 'No!' they said. 'We want a king over us. Then we shall be like all the other nations, with a king to lead us and to go out before us and fight our battles.'*

*When Samuel heard all that the people said, he repeated it before the LORD. The LORD answered, 'Listen to them and give them a king.'*                              (1 Samuel 8:1–22)

Can you believe it? Pretty specific, eh?

The Lord clearly described the consequences of having a human king instead of Himself and they were extensive, clear and wholly unpleasant. But the problem was that God had given man authority and dominion on the earth and He hadn't changed His mind, whatever man's choices or the consequences. He had to accede to their wishes, but in His mercy warned them of what would happen.

It seems unbelievable that they would choose the oppression of man rather than the blessing of God. Remember, these were the children of Israel, the people of God who knew what God required and what was required of them. Again and again we read of their choices to serve other gods, despite knowing what God had said.

Today, as we seek to play our part in establishing God's kingdom on earth, we need to be aware of the inherent flaw within mankind to reject God as King even if the cost is personal and extensive in our own lives. Our fallen selves have a seed of rebellion which needs to be purged from our hearts and minds so that the kingdom can come and rule.

We need both the *logos* and *rhema* word impacting our lives; we need a prophetic revelation of who our King is and how to be kingdom people.

We need the prophetic in our lives to help us see hear and understand how to embrace and establish His kingdom in our lives, churches, communities, nations and generations.

Our very lives are a prophetic statement, a message which shows that man really can be reconciled to God and administer His rule and reign on earth, as it is in heaven.

As it was in the beginning, so it shall be today.

# Dethroning Our Kings

> For though we live in the world, we do not wage war as the world does. The weapons we fight with are not the weapons of the world. On the contrary, they have divine power to demolish strongholds. We demolish arguments and every pretension that sets itself up against the knowledge of God, and we take captive every thought to make it obedient to Christ.
>
> (2 Corinthians 10:3–5)

Kings in our lives can overrule and obstruct God's purposes in and through us. Kings require subjects and we will be drawn to subject our own selves to serve our 'king', be it ambition, desire, material possessions, recognition, social or cultural expectations, habit or even ministry!

The main king we are to dethrone is our own 'flesh king' that wants to rule over the spirit within us. Our thoughts can dominate us, tormenting us with attempts to rule our mind and behaviour. Most people would find that the major 'king' is in the area of the mind. Mental illness is the most dominant infirmity facing those in the Western world. US statistics indicate that more than fifty-four million Americans suffer from mental illness in any one year (*SGRMH* 1999 – *Surgeon General's Report on Mental Health*). Nineteen million suffer from depression or anxiety, one per cent of the American population suffer from schizophrenia (*Schizophrenia Bulletin* 1998), manic depression affects more than two million Americans (NIMH 2000 – National Institute of Mental Health).

Earthly 'kings', including our own flesh ones, struggle with the 'priest' and 'prophet' function in our lives, as our thinking and behaviour are challenged by our spirits, in order that the true King can be served. This is our true and valid desire as Christians, but we struggle. As Paul said, '*Who will rescue* [us] *from this body of death?*' (Romans 7:24).

When we live in our prophetic and priestly anointing we move in the wisdom, revelation and function that enables us to live rightly, righteously, before God. When we do this there is no room for any other king than the King of kings.

As *priests* we present ourselves before God, as living sacrifices and we present others on earth through our priestly prayers of authority and faith.

As *prophets* we hear from God and communicate what we hear on earth.

*Prayer and prophecy* – the priestly and prophetic functions of God's people on earth. All of us are called to both pray and speak forth the words of God. Jesus called us to *preach the gospel of the kingdom* (see Matthew 24:14).

All God's people are called to carry a prophetic and priestly role on earth. As Father's children we hear God's voice to us as a loving Father. As servants of the King we need to be open and attentive to our Master's voice. As ambassadors for Christ we need to receive instruction to re-present Him on earth in accordance with heaven's purpose and protocol.

As members of the Church, His Body, we need to hear and speak to build up and encourage the people of God, helping them hear, understand and align with His will on earth, as it is in heaven. These are all prophetic roles and functions that every child of God is called and able to do.

We dethrone our kings as we live in these prophetic and priestly roles, submitting to Him humbly and with a heart to maintain peace and unity, but serving one Master in all that we do. He has priority in our heads and lives and this is the tension we face on earth as we are called to honour and prefer one another. Many people get confused about the balance between humble submission and being overly controlled by others. This is probably the biggest challenge and danger in the Body of Christ and one that often causes strife and division. We must seek the Lord for wisdom, revelation and strategies so we are a blessing to one another, not allowing fear of man to control us.

Time spent in prayer and fasting can be invaluable in preparing and positioning ourselves, giving room for the Holy Spirit to work in us, changing us, revealing God's heart and mind on a matter, giving us wisdom and strategies, peace and rest.

## What happens when a king is dethroned?

There's a bit of a shock!

Everything we've become familiar with is subject to a radical change of authority. There's a sense of loss as change is difficult for humans. Studies on the management of change advise awareness that there needs to be a practical action plan to enable the change to be effected smoothly, with minimum disruption.

We need to go through the period of putting off the old attitudes, behaviours and expectations in order to embrace new ways of thinking and acting. As Paul says, 'We need to take every thought captive to make it obedient to Christ' (see 2 Corinthians 10:5). Jesus doesn't deceive or deny the truth, rather He exhorts us to count the cost before we make choices and decisions (see Luke 14).

There is a cost to change. There is usually a battle to overthrow a king. But we have the promises of God:

- We have armour to wear (Ephesians 6:13)

- We have words of wisdom that no adversary can resist (Luke 21:14–15)
- We have the promise that He will rescue us from our enemies (Luke 1:73–75)
- We have authority to be overcomers (Luke 10:18–20)
- We can overcome evil with good (Romans 12:20–21)
- *We are born of God*:

> *This is love for God: to obey his commands. And his commands are not burdensome, for everyone born of God overcomes the world. This is the victory that has overcome the world, even our faith. Who is it that overcomes the world? Only he who believes that Jesus is the Son of God.*　　　　　　　(1 John 5:3–5)

# CHAPTER 3

# The Kingdom Place

Jesus said a lot about the kingdom.

What does 'kingdom' mean?

There are a number of theological views on the subject of 'kingdom'. This book is not about a theological debate. It is about seeking a right response in how we live on earth as people who are called to be priests in the kingdom, ambassadors for the King and prophets who proclaim the kingdom has come to earth.

So the kingdom has a number of expressions through God's people on earth.

## What is the kingdom of God?

It is in this world and the world to come.

It has come to earth through Jesus' work in redeeming all things back to the Father.

It is where the eternal sovereign God rules over all things (see Psalm 103:19).

It is universal, eternal and spiritual.

## Kingdom distinctives

The existence of a kingdom supposes the following:

- That there is a King in rightful rule over the kingdom

- That there are decrees by which the will of the King is administered
- That there are subjects in the kingdom
- That there are those who have roles and responsibilities to carry out the rule of the King
- That there are distinctives which identify the kingdom people, identity, culture and values.

## Kingdom manifest

Jesus is the King of our kingdom. He is the King over every king that ever was, is or will be.

There is one law which rules this kingdom. It is a law which requires perfect holiness, through worship and obedience to the King.

Jesus fulfilled all the Old Testament Law in His atonement – in other words He took the place of sacrifice for us so that we can be found blameless before God.

This is a difficult concept for the human mind to grasp.

Jesus described what fulfilment of the Law really meant in Matthew 22 – The Greatest Commandment:

> *Hearing that Jesus had silenced the Sadducees, the Pharisees got together. One of them, an expert in the law, tested him with this question: 'Teacher, which is the greatest commandment in the Law?'*
>
> *Jesus replied: ' "Love the Lord your God with all your heart and with all your soul and with all your mind." This is the first and greatest commandment. And the second is like it: "Love your neighbour as yourself." All the Law and the Prophets hang on these two commandments.'*                          (Matthew 22:34–40)

This law is now written on our hearts – by His Spirit.

It is only the Spirit of God who can fulfil the law of the Kingdom. There is absolutely nothing we can do in ourselves to fulfil the law. Our best efforts will always fall short.

Paul challenged the Jewish believers in Galatia when they tried to make Gentile converts to abide by some Old Testament rites. He said that they were 'bewitched' as they had lost the truth that the Spirit alone in us can obey God's laws and that the Spirit can only be received by 'faith'.

---

**Faith or observance of the law**

*You foolish Galatians! Who has bewitched you? Before your very eyes Jesus Christ was clearly portrayed as crucified. I would like to learn just one thing from you: Did you receive the Spirit by observing the law, or by believing what you heard? Are you so foolish? After beginning with the Spirit, are you now trying to attain your goal by human effort? Have you suffered so much for nothing – if it really was for nothing? Does God give you his Spirit and work miracles among you because you observe the law, or because you believe what you heard?* (Galatians 3:1–5)

---

You see it is too simple for human perception to grasp. It can only be discerned through the Spirit working within us.

We really cannot do anything in ourselves to meet God's criteria. So He has given us His very Spirit to come and do the work in us.

## Citizens of the kingdom

All those who are born of the Spirit enter the kingdom as citizens.

---

*Consequently, you are no longer foreigners and aliens, but fellow-citizens with God's people and members of God's household, built on the foundation of the apostles and prophets, with Christ Jesus himself as the chief cornerstone. In him the whole building is joined together and rises to become a holy temple in the Lord. And in him you too are being built together to become a dwelling in which God lives by his Spirit.* (Ephesians 2:19–22)

---

We are subjects of the King with roles and responsibilities as part of our citizenship.

The evidence of the kingdom on earth is a people who are both a nation of priests and prophets, who represent their King in word and deed with signs and wonders as a consequence of the kingdom revealed and released on earth – as it is in heaven.

We are called to *be* and *do* in our kingdom roles.

We represent the King by the way we our lives on earth and also we are expected to proclaim the kingdom. This is our priestly and prophetic job description.

A priestly and prophetic anointing are the kingly garments we wear, which mark us out among the peoples of the earth.

## We are called as priests of the Lord – a kingdom of priests

When the Lord prophesied the call out of Egypt He declared His intention that the people would be a kingdom of priests and a holy nation for God. This is the essence of the life we are called to live today. We have priestly roles and responsibilities to stand before man on behalf of God with another anointing, a prophetic anointing, to hear the Lord and speak on His behalf.

Under the Old Covenant the priestly and prophetic roles were few and they were the only ones who could function in these roles. Under the New Covenant we have the fullness of Christ and have that *double* portion which Isaiah prophesied:

> And you will be called priests of the LORD,
>     you will be named ministers of our God.
> You will feed on the wealth of nations,
>     and in their riches you will boast.
> Instead of their shame
>     my people will receive a double portion,
> and instead of disgrace
>     they will rejoice in their inheritance;
> and so they will inherit a double portion in their land,
>     and everlasting joy will be theirs.          (Isaiah 61:6–7)

## Kingdom come

> *Jesus said, 'My kingdom is not of this world. If it were, my servants would fight to prevent my arrest by the Jews. But now my kingdom is from another place.'*
>
> *'You are a king, then!' said Pilate.*
>
> *Jesus answered, 'You are right in saying I am a king. In fact, for this reason I was born, and for this I came into the world, to testify to the truth.'* (John 18:36 – 37)

The kingdom of God is not of this world. But it has *come* to this world. It has come through a message, a word – that message was a Person.

It still is today.

It is you. You are the person who carries the message. You are a kingdom carrier. The truth of the Father who sent His Son to do His will so that He could give His kingdom to people on earth who could see and respond to that truth. The Father is so excited about you and me having the kingdom. So it's not a place – it's a gift. It's inside of us and it's longing to be released.

## The Parables of the Mustard Seed and the Yeast

> *Then Jesus asked, 'What is the kingdom of God like? What shall I compare it to? It is like a mustard seed, which a man took and planted in his garden. It grew and became a tree, and the birds of the air perched in its branches.'*
>
> *Again he asked, 'What shall I compare the kingdom of God to? It is like yeast that a woman took and mixed into a large amount of flour until it worked all through the dough.'* (Luke 13:18 – 21)

For the kingdom extends and grows as we release it through our lives and words. Jesus said it's like a mustard seed that grows so big that it's like a tree that attracts birds to nest in it. It's like a tiny piece of yeast that can grow into a great loaf.

How will anyone know unless we give the message?

We can only receive the message if we receive it like a child (see Luke 18:17). So we don't need complicated, fancy ways of communicating.

We just need a simple message. A life message. It's not a message of just words from human mouths. This message has power behind it. When we talk about the kingdom, the very power of God is behind out words. Heaven gets excited to hear kingdom words on earth (see 1 Corinthians 4:20).

The kingdom is nothing like a kingdom in this world. It's not about food and drink.

You'll know it when you see it because righteousness, peace and joy are there (see Romans 14:17).

## The kingdom commission

As citizens of the kingdom we are commissioned to go out, i.e. beyond the boundaries of the current kingdom, and preach the kingdom of God (see Luke 9:1–3).

Jesus' ministry was about proclaiming the kingdom (see Matthew 4:23).

Whenever He did this there was a manifestation of power and a powerful response. The response was either acceptance or rejection of the kingdom.

## The kingdom complete

> *Then the end will come, when he hands over the kingdom to God the Father after he has destroyed all dominion, authority and power.*          (1 Corinthians 15:24)

We're on a commission to serve our King in extending the kingdom. As the kingdom is extended so the dominion and power of the usurper on earth will be destroyed. It is an exciting time to live on earth. We must have the eyes of Joshua and Caleb to look into the land and see the promises of God. We are not battling against an enemy with equal power to God. We are battling on behalf of the King who has all power in heaven and earth. We do not go out in our own strength, but the power of the Spirit of God will enable us to be kingdom people who are humble in their own eyes but confident in their King.

The end is all about the King's desire to please His Father.

His Father wants restoration. Restoration to His children.

Our kingdom call is to *extend* the kingdom to the ends of the earth.

> *He says, It is too light a thing that you should be My servant to raise up the tribes of Jacob and to restore the survivors [of the judgments] of Israel; I will also give you for a light to the nations, that My salvation may extend to the end of the earth.*      (Isaiah 49:6 AMP)

# PART 2

## *On Words and Wisdom*

# Prophets and Priests

> 'Now if you obey me fully and keep my covenant, then out of all
> nations you will be my treasured possession. Although the whole
> earth is mine, you will be for me a kingdom of priests and a holy
> nation.' These are the words you are to speak to the Israelites.
> So Moses went back and summoned the elders of the people and
> set before them all the words the Lᴏʀᴅ had commanded him to
> speak.                                               (Exodus 19:5 – 7)

As we saw in Chapter 1, God's plan between the Fall and the
coming of the Messiah was an interim plan to restore relationship
and communication between Himself and His creation. He
ordained priests and prophets to fulfil the two significant roles and
functions which would ensure two-way communication for God's
word to be received and for the people to respond.

Priests were ordained to represent man to God. Prophets were
anointed to represent God to man. The people of God were all to be
a priestly kingdom, living a life of obedience to God, representing
and modelling a relationship with God based on clear direction for
every area of their lives. As God's people obeyed Him and lived in
accordance to His direction, so abundant blessing would be the
consequence.

There was perfect two-way communication between God and

man through the ministry of the prophet and the priest. The prophet, hearing and speaking for God, the priest responding to God's word and representing the people to Him.

We are all called to be both prophets and priests on earth today. We are all called to hear God's voice and respond to what He says, in obedience. Jesus was very clear that His disciples are those who don't just hear the word – but those who actually do what God says.

## Prophetic problems

'The true purpose of prophecy is to build up, admonish and stir up, encourage and release from pain and discomfort, and to enable people to know and understand the heartbeat of God for them-selves. If it doesn't achieve that, it is not true prophecy.'

(Graham Cooke)

As we travel in our prophetic ministry it is astonishing how many people tell us of the catalogues of prophetic words they have received. Many of these words are quite specific and speak of God's promises and blessings. It is equally astonishing how many people put these words on a shelf to gather dust until God 'makes them happen'. There is a kind of unwritten assumption, even theology, implied in this way of thinking. Of course, every word needs to be weighed, judged and tested to see if it is indeed a true word from God. However, there is a subtle, but extremely significant, difference between waiting on the Lord for the time of fulfilment and responding in faith to the word.

I'll be very clear and say that we cannot make a prophetic word happen. But I will say, equally strongly, that we can prevent a personal prophetic word coming to pass. Just as it is God's will that no one should perish, we know that many will. So it is with prophetic words. We can receive or reject them. There needs to be wisdom and understanding to know what to do with a prophetic word that is received.

God will have a time, season and purpose for that word to be fulfilled (see Ecclesiastes 4). We have a responsibility to live in accordance with that word, so we are prepared when it is time for it to come to pass.

For example, it is not unusual for someone to come up to me at an event and ask for prayer. They will often say that they have words about being 'called to the nations'. They then hint, or hope, for me to prophesy over them about this word. They also probably ask a number of prophetic people to do the same, seeking ever more confirmation of the word.

But at some point *each person* has to make his or her own response. Each person needs to consider, given all the confirmation, witness and peace he or she has over the word, what his or her response is. You see, it doesn't matter if fifty prophets all agree that the word is true, nothing is likely to happen unless a person makes a decision to *receive* the word into his or her own heart. You see, when the word says 'faith comes from *hearing* the word of God' (see Romans 10:17), it is not just the physical 'hearing' that is the issue, it's whether that person 'heard' in his or her heart and allowed the truth – the 'seed' – go in and take root. The Parable of the Sower is very clear about the various consequences of the word being sown. The word can fall on the stony ground of hard hearts, or be choked by the thistles of cares in this world, or dry up due to the sandy ground that does not have the substance to hold the word.

I remember a young girl asking me to pray for her as she was 'called to Africa'. She wanted to work with young babies in an orphanage. While this is a commendable attitude I wanted to find out a bit more before praying. We can sometimes pray too quickly in response to human desire, when the Lord may have a different agenda for a person's life! In this case I spent some time asking her which part of Africa she felt called to as it is a large continent! She didn't know. I asked her if she knew anyone already working there who could give her advice or counsel about how to prepare to go out. She didn't. I asked her if she planned any training to look after children or babies. She didn't.

I suggested that before praying to be sent out she had a part to play in getting herself ready to fulfil the call she believed was on her life. I suggested she might like to start by 'sowing where she wanted to go'. In other words, providing prayer or financial support to someone who was already doing what she felt called to do. I suggested she might spend some time taking appropriate training for working with children, so that she would be an immediate blessing to those she sought to serve. I suggested she might plan some short-term mission to Africa in order to become culturally and practically aware of the conditions in which she would be working.

She was supremely unimpressed with my 'prophetic ministry'. She told me in no uncertain terms 'I only asked you to pray!'

If you told that story to anyone working in missions they could tell you similar stories of people who had 'felt called' to go out and help on the mission field with a romantic idea of what that would be like. Often these people become a burden instead of a blessing and take the key workers away from their call to minister to their distress.

While it may have been true that this was part of the Lord's call on a life, it is also true that we must play our part in preparing ourselves, counting the cost and paying the price.

He never said it would be easy, but He did say He would always be with us and He does send His power to accomplish His purposes in and through us.

When the word of God comes to us, it doesn't just come to give us a warm feeling inside. Luke 1:37 in the Amplified Bible is a wonderful expression of what accompanies the word: *'no word from God shall be without power or impossible of fulfillment'*. When we receive His word we have the power in us to carry it out.

## Two for the price of one!

We get two for the price of one when we get a word from God! Every word He speaks has, inextricably embedded within it, the very power of God. How awesome is that!

Imagine a seed from an ear of corn, one seed. Unseen, contained within that seed is the power to become a field of corn, a harvest, food for a nation. Yet, unless that seed is planted and tended in right conditions, nothing will happen. That one seed has unlimited potential to grow, multiply and go on being reproduced for generations. That is the purpose for that seed. It doesn't exist to be a small, dry seed but it has purpose way beyond itself.

So how much more is the word that God speaks over our lives. A word from God has inherent power not only to fulfil its divine destiny and purpose in our individual lives on earth, but also to reproduce and impact in manifold ways beyond the here and now. Any word from God has an eternal prospect as well as an earthly one. We do not know the extent of God's words to us. They are truly intended to be 'more than we can ask, think or imagine' (see Ephesians 3:20). Everything God creates is made for abundantly more than itself.

What about the words over your life? What about your God-given hopes and dreams? Where are they? Are they still in your hand, yet to be sown in your heart, watered and tended so they will grow? Did you not realise that you had a part to play because once God's word comes to earth, He expects mankind to pick it up and sow it? The heavens He made for Himself but the earth is given to man (see Psalm 115:16). When God ordains something on earth He restrains Himself until man responds.

The first response is always a choice – a faith choice. The choice is to believe or question God's meaning – just like Adam. Did God really say . . . ?

You see, not only do we get two for the price of one – the power of God accompanying every word He speaks. We also get faith *as* we receive the word of God. Faith comes by hearing – hearing in our hearts, receiving the word, letting it take root (see Romans 10:17).

So we get the word, plus power and then faith. What more do we need? When we get faith we get assurance that it will come to pass. We don't need to continually seek confirmation or more prophetic words when faith has come. We need the words *so that* faith can come. Once it's come it's a done deal in our hearts.

The next step is to tend the word, watering it and watching over it. Remember Mary – she received the word (even though it was at enormous personal cost to herself) and made a decision to receive it (by saying 'Yes' to the angel) and then she pondered it in her heart. She kept it alive and real to herself. She would have been preparing her heart, mind, will and emotions to deal with the fulfilment of that word.

What's the difference with words we receive? These principles are the same for any word we get.

So how about those words over your life? Have you received them in your heart? You do have a choice, you know.

## A word of warning

It wouldn't be fair of me to suggest that the next step is to receive the word. It's not. The next step is to consider whether you *want* to receive the word. You see, Jesus was very clear and very fair about the consequences of our choices. He said no one sets about to build a building without first counting the cost.

If we realise the truth that when God speaks any word into our lives it has more significance, impact and consequence than even the grandest building ever built on earth, then we will consider His prophetic revelation with sober reflection and considered response. It has more significance than we could ever think or imagine and it has impact into eternity.

God's word and words are eternal and they all have eternal significance.

We just can't think or imagine the awesomeness – so we think and imagine that they are just for the 'here and now' of life on earth.

If a single seed has the potential to feed nations and generations, how much more potential has a word of God spoken to an individual on earth?

## Prophets – living the word on earth

*Behold, how good and how pleasant it is for brethren to dwell together in unity!*

*It is like the precious ointment poured on the head, that ran down on the beard, even the beard of Aaron ... that came down upon the collar and skirts of his garments ...*

*It is like the dew of [lofty] Mount Hermon, and the dew that comes on the hills of Zion; for there the Lord has commanded the blessing, even life for evermore.* (Psalm 133:1–3 AMP)

*'That all of them may be one, Father, just as you are in me and I am in you. May they also be in us so that the world may believe that you have sent me. I have given them the glory that you gave me, that they may be one as we are one: I in them and you in me. May they be brought to complete unity to let the world know that you sent me and have loved them even as you have loved me.'* (John 17:21–23)

What is a prophet? One who proclaims what is to come.

All of us can ask the Holy Spirit for the gift of prophecy. It is the privilege of every believer to be able to move in the gift.

There are also those who have been called to function primarily in the prophetic ministry. In these days I believe it is a priority for the prophets in the nations to begin to recognise and respond to one another, modelling Jesus' desire that we 'dwell together in unity'. This means taking time out from personal agendas to be inconvenienced by the joy and challenge of building relationally. The prophetic function can be a popular and demanding one, leaving little time or opportunity to build with others.

## General aspects of prophetic function

- Gifted with the spiritual gift of prophecy
- Positioned and prepared to hear God's voice
- Ability to discern, interpret and communicate God's word
- Willing to pay the price in living the word
- Understanding the 'time and season' for the word

The prophetic is meant to prepare the way, with 'prophets' being a living example of the prophecy we proclaim in the way we live our lives. We need to have faith for fulfilment of the prophetic word and that faith will be seen in our choices and decisions.

I believe there is an urgency in the heavens to see the prophets come together, preferring and honouring one another, modelling and influencing the church to prepare a people and a place for the word of God to come and dwell in the church.

It is crucial that we understand the powerful and holy message that is conveyed as we 'dwell together in unity'. This is such a familiar phrase we can miss the vital importance of the unity message which is conveyed in living in the 'one-ness' we are in Christ. Paul urges us to live at peace with one another, as far as it depends on us. Our enemy will always try to accuse, condemn, judge and divide us and as we are tempted to do the same we can do the enemy's work for him. As we live out of hearts and actions that demonstrate this unity we will truly be a sign and a symbol to the world that will cause the world to know and believe.

As we choose unity, we dethrone our ego, personal agenda and self-will as an act of service and sacrifice to God, choosing a different way of living from the way of the world and our flesh. We will demonstrate our love for God and man as we walk the way of unity.

## Priests – representing man to God

> *Then the priests, the Levites, arose and blessed the people, and their voice was heard; and their prayer came up to His holy dwelling place, to heaven.* (2 Chronicles 30:27 NKJV)

What is a priest? Someone who is anointed and set apart to serve the Lord and administer His will on earth.

We have a wonderful role as priests on earth and our prayers have impact and significance in life on earth. Jesus was very clear that we have our part to play on earth to receive the blessings and provision of God as well as act in partnership with Him to see His purposes and plans released on earth. He even said that we would do greater works than He did (see John 14:12)!

## General aspects of priesthood

- Anointed for service
- 'Set apart', identified as a point of contact on earth to intercede for man
- Communicating to God on behalf of the people
- Making disciples
- Ministering to the Body of Christ

All of these prophetic and priestly aspects support the Great Commission, which is the calling to every follower of Christ. We are in the world, but not of it.

If you are reading this book as a follower of Christ then each of these applies to you:

- *You* are anointed by the Holy Spirit, who is ever present within and alongside you, to help you, teach you and communicate the Father's will to you (John 15:26)
- *You* are set apart yet called to be Christ's witness on earth, salt and light, bringing Christ to the people around you (Matthew 5:13)

- *You* are called to pray and intercede for those on earth (1 Timothy 2:1)
- *You* are commissioned to make disciples, teach, heal … Whatever it takes to enable believers to become disciples (Matthew 28:19)
- *You* are called to minister Christ to others, discover and move in your gift and calling, playing your part in the Body, so that the whole church can grow and mature (Ephesians 4:13)

## Prophetic solutions

We are sometimes asked to advise individuals or churches on what to do with prophetic words. It is exciting, interesting and saddening to see various responses to our advice. Yet there are quite simple, obvious things to do with a word that comes. You see, we can make prophetic words so mystical and mysterious that they are 'not of this world'. In fact, although they are eternal, while they are on earth there will be a very practical, down-to-earth process of working through to fulfilment.

There are three distinct decisions, which will impact the fulfilment of any prophetic word, individual or corporate. Just like a natural seed, a prophetic word has a time, season, purpose and place for it to grow, flourish and fulfil its purpose.

- *Decision 1: Receiving the word* – accepting it as a true message from God. This assumes proper, scriptural weighing and judging the word, with confirmation through witnesses (see 1 Thessalonians 5:20–21; 1 John 4:1–3).
- *Decision 2: Believing the word* – allowing the word to enter the heart with the consequence that faith will come as we believe (see Romans 10:17).
- *Decision 3: Releasing the word* – living in expectation of fulfilment of the word, making any changes or actions in line with the word.

# Receiving the Word

> 'Today, if you hear his voice,
>     do not harden your hearts.'
> (Hebrews 3:7)
>
> *The natural, nonspiritual man does not accept or welcome or admit into his heart the gifts and teachings and revelations of the Spirit of God, for they are folly (meaningless nonsense) to him ... because they are spiritually discerned.* (1 Corinthians 2:14 AMP)

Before we consider how to receive a prophetic word we need to identify exactly what we mean by a 'word'. Many of us have limited our ability to hear and receive because we have set ideas based on understanding or experience within our church culture or background. The truth is that God is truth and He will not be confined to our limits, but is ever present, loving us by His Spirit – forever 'speaking' to us and desiring that we, His beloved, respond.

We are called to actually *live* by every word that comes from God's mouth (Matthew 4:4). The Bible feeds us with prophetic revelation, as we allow the Spirit of God to speak to our hearts through the written word. The prophetic gift in us will respond to the 'voice' of God as we live 'in tune', alert and expecting to hear Him speak. Even the law was a spiritual declaration of God's plan for restoration to relationship with Him. Our God requires His people to be holy and this comes through hearing and obeying

His word, not by following religious ritual. The rituals were symbolic of the relational truth of God's people getting in right relationship with Him.

## What is this thing called 'prophecy'?

'Prophecy is a gift and a ministry that we should encourage to the uttermost in our churches. A lot of the misconceptions on prophecy arise out of a lack of knowledge and understanding about what it is, how it works and the way in which we should release it into the local church.'
(Graham Cooke)

Prophecy is a communication of God's heart, mind, will or emotions to individuals, groups, nations or generations. It originates with God, is revealed to us and released on earth, through a response in word or deed. Prophecy *always* requires a response. Our spirits are designed to recognise the voice of God. Our souls (mind, will and emotions) are *subject* to our spirits and we need to take care that we discern the word of God in our spirits. An emotional response, or feeling, may, or may not, be an indication that the word is from God. Our flesh will want to interpret the word in line with our own desires and needs. Discernment is crucial for anyone wishing to receive or give prophetic revelation. Many people get confused if they don't get the same 'feeling' as the previous time they had a prophetic word, or if it doesn't come in the same way. What they are really wanting is for God to fit their own 'image' and not being open to let God be God and speak how and when He wants. When we try to understand God, yet limit our ability to hear and receive, we are denying ourselves the exciting, abundant life that Jesus came to give us.

Our God is a *big* God. His word caused the whole of creation to burst into the perfect reality of His plans and evermore will continue in unfolding beauty and wonder. God's purpose for us is eternal, yet in our smallness we make limitations on His impact into our lives. We have made prophecy too small, isolated and safe in our management of what we receive. God can and will speak as He chooses and our absolute priority is to hear His voice and do what He says. One thing is sure – when He speaks that same creation power will accompany every word, enabling us, if we will respond, to co-operate with Him to bring His kingdom to earth.

> *For with God nothing is ever impossible and no word from God shall be without power or impossible of fulfillment.*     (Luke 1:37 AMP)

So, if every word from God has power for fulfilment, why are there unfulfilled words? There are many reasons for this, which we will look at later.

## The communication factor

What is important is that we understand that communication results from a relational connection with another person. Communication requires at least two 'people' to send and receive a message. Communication is central to our lives. It 'connects' us with others; assures us we are not alone; enables us to express meaning. God is a relational being. He is three-in-one, three persons: Father, Son and Holy Spirit. Each person communicates, hears, honours, blesses and impacts the other. What an awesome God we serve, with loving relationship at the centre of His being. What an awesome place we have, centred in the middle of that relationship. Imagine Father, Son and Holy Spirit circling us with their arms of love, holding us and releasing waves of love and words of affirmation to us. This is the reality of life in the Spirit. We are with Christ in the spiritual realm, seated with Him, yet present on earth to do His will. We are both spiritual and natural beings – just like He was.

Communication is more than words – it's an expression from 'one' to 'another'. An expression of meaning or intention, demonstrated through a myriad of ways, not just words, but acts of kindness, sacrifice, art, drama, music and endless other ways.

## Message received?

Successful communication occurs when the message transmitted by the sender is received with the *intended* message clear and intact. Sounds simple. God speaks, we hear. Message sent: message received. However, frequently there are distortions to the original message as it passes along the communication routes. The old, familiar anecdote from the World War I is often quoted as an example of extreme distortion of the original communication. A message was being passed along the line to say – 'Send reinforcements, we are going to advance'. By the time the message had passed down the line it had changed to 'Send three and four pence, we are going to a dance'!

So it can be with prophetic revelation. The original word may be clear and accurate, but other factors come into play to distort the purpose and meaning to make it almost unintelligible. Often the receivers' own agendas will interpret the word in line with current desires or needs, so that everything they 'hear' will line up with their own wishes. Whenever we receive a word, we must be aware that this is not just a 'prophetic word' to launch into someone's life, but that God has a specific purpose and meaning in giving the word and our job is to make sure it is given in the best possible way, time and attitude to ensure minimum distortion of God's intention. I say, minimum, because we live on earth, in our flesh bodies, and we only ever see 'in part' (see 1 Corinthians 13:9).

Our preferred 'style' of giving a word may be good for us, but the receiver may not appreciate or understand our way and lose some of the meaning along the way. I once received an accurate, powerful and timely prophetic word from someone who was known for a particular 'shouting' style of prophecy, with plenty of 'Thus sayeth the Lord', 'Yea, verilys' and each sentence repeated at least twice. My natural inclination would be to switch off as I'm a 'down-to-earth' kind of prophetic person, but I realised that this word was probably one of the most significant words I'd ever had, although wrapped up in Olde English and a weird presentation style. I made a choice, not to switch off, but to 'hear' God through the barriers of language and style. While it was good that I chose to hear, it would have been much easier if the word had been given in a simple, easy to understand way. It's not difficult to consider the 'audience' for the word and make an effort to ensure the word is given in an appropriate way for *them* to hear, not in a style, which may be more about creating an impact than ensuring the word lands safely!

## Ears to hear?

> 'One of the things we need to move in prophecy is a burden and a concern. It's burden that reveals God's heart. When we have a burden for something and we're praying, the Holy Spirit enables us to put that into words and we begin to feel that God wants to say and do something.' (Graham Cooke)

Jesus caused some confusion to His disciples and followers through His parables. He would say, 'He who has ears to hear, let him hear.' He was really saying, 'Look guys, you are trying to work out what I'm saying in your natural thinking. You can't. Spiritual things need to be spiritually discerned. You need to think differently, so you can get what I'm talking about' (see 1 Corinthians 2:14). Of course, the disciples had not yet received the Holy Spirit and had limitations on their 'discern-ability'! It does give us a clue though, that just being with Jesus isn't enough, and we need to draw on the Holy Spirit within us to help us discern God's word to us.

## Hearing into faith

When we do hear and discern God's word a spiritual transformation takes place. Faith is released to us and in us as the word is planted in our hearts. Faith comes for that word to be fulfilled. All believers have faith *in* God but we also need specific faith for specific purposes. I find that faith for specific things is a bit like the manna in the wilderness. You need fresh faith for each specific thing. We can have a consistent faith *in* God, that He is who He says He is and that He will do what He says He will do. But when it comes to specific challenges, we can struggle to believe. That's the wonderful thing about prophecy. Someone can come along with a specific word, which impacts a situation or challenge, speaking hope or encouragement, direction or correction and that word can provoke faith in us to help us in that situation. Faith is the 'fruit' of our response to the word of God. It comes. When we don't have it, we can get it (see Romans 10:17).

It's interesting that faith comes to the saved and unsaved. For it is while we are unsaved that the word of life comes to us. As we respond, receiving the 'word', so faith is ignited in our hearts and we are able to believe in Him. Faith is the consequence of hearing.

## Identifying the source

While it is clear that we can hear the voice of the Father, we live in a world full of other voices which are constantly competing for our attention. It requires a disciplined approach to listening and responding in order to discern the source of the words we hear.

Even when a true word is discerned, we will have to consider the influence of the other voices in interpreting and applying the word in our lives.

The three main common 'voices' we hear are:

| The world | The flesh | The devil |
|-----------|-----------|-----------|
| *Culture* | *Soul* | *Accuser* |
| Experience | Mind | Shame |
| Society | Will | Fear |
| Values | Emotions | Pain |

Our culture can influence how we receive words. If our culture values success and material acquisition as 'good' then we will find it difficult to hear a call to a fasted, sacrificial lifestyle. Or if we do hear it we may interpret it within the cultural context, e.g. giving up TV for a season or missing the odd meal.

Culture can also influence how we give words. We are all aware of the different 'styles' of prophecy which reflect national or denominational cultures. We are from a Pentecostal background where there were obvious signs accompanying the giving of a word – usually with passionate, loud repetition. This is not wrong in itself, but it is just a cultural expression. The issue is whether those from such a culture could recognise a word which is given in an informal, gentle way.

Our souls have a vested interest in hearing and responding to what fits our human frame of reference. Our minds will try and work out the logic of a word, our wills want the word to fit our own plans and our emotions will react to what our mind and will stir up in us!

Finally, we have the 'Accuser of the Brethren' who is hell bent on preventing the word of God being released on earth. He knows only too well that any word from God has the power of God attached to it. He also knows that God entrusts His words to His people and gives us freedom to handle them. The enemy has always been passionately resolute in determination to kill the prophetic words by attacking those who have a call to release the word. He knows the power of shame, fear and pain to prevent people having the confidence in their own call and anointing to be ministers for God's word.

## Dealing with the voices

### The world

We need wisdom and revelation of the truth that, although we are in the world, we are no longer part of its culture and control. We cannot be friends with the world's ways. This was the error the children of Israel made when they compromised to accommodate the world's ways, which have always been in opposition to God's purposes. Jesus' prayer is our confidence that the Father will protect us in the world (see John 17:13–18).

## The flesh

We are new creations, no longer needing to be controlled by our old ways as we have the Spirit of God in us, to lead and teach us in all things. In ourselves we can do nothing, but with the Spirit we can do all things. We can take every though captive to obedience to Christ (see John 14:26; 2 Corinthians 5:17; 10:5; Philippians 4:13).

## The devil

Our position when facing the devil is one of being covered and clothed in Christ Himself. We need to be alert and aware of the enemy's intention to steal, kill and destroy anything that brings the glory, kingdom and power of God to earth. He will tempt us just like he tempted Jesus. He knows the Scriptures and will have a strategy to challenge us with them. We need to study the Scriptures so we are not ignorant of their truth and power. We are told to resist the devil and he will flee. We must make sure we don't have any place where he can have his foothold (see Ephesians 4:27; 6:11; James 4:7; 1 Peter 5:8).

## Discernment

'The gift of discerning of spirits enables us to determine the spiritual origin or source of actual events, or the spoken word. There can be an immediate witness in my spirit. This must be confirmed in other ways too; by Scripture and by agreement with people of maturity. Where there is no inner witness to prophecy, we must exercise caution, attempting to discover the following: Is the source of the word an evil spirit? Is the word originating out of this person's human sprit? Is it the spirit of man?'        (Graham Cooke)

Discernment is one of the gifts of the Spirit. It is the ability to know the spirit behind what is said or what appears. It is not about looking at things logically, analytically, culturally or soulishly. Christians need to draw on the Holy Spirit to 'hear' and 'know' what God's truth reveals. Jesus always declares the Good News – the New Covenant is not of the law but of the Spirit; for the law kills but the Spirit gives *life* (see 2 Corinthians 3:6).

We are all saints – walking in the Spirit. But we also find our old selves emerge from time to time. Sometimes prophecies start in the Spirit and end in the flesh. Sometimes they are just flesh! These may come from good intentions but they are not prophecies from the Holy Spirit. If you discern this when receiving a word – do not respond. Just pray and renounce the word being spoken.

Words have power and we have the discernment of the Holy Spirit as a safety net. If you discern something wrong being said over you then you have the power to stop it entering your heart, mind, spirit, will or emotions.

### What do we discern?

Revelation 19:10 tells us that the essence of the truth revealed by Jesus is the spirit of all prophecy. All that Jesus is, has done, has planned, desires and communicates is what is prophesied and the benchmark by which we discern. Does the revelation reveal Jesus?

The Spirit gives *life* (2 Corinthians 3:6) – so we ask does this revelation give life (even if it is correction which is for our good), or is it accusing/condemning?

Our spirits, renewed and redeemed by the Holy Spirit, respond to the true word of God. We do not discern by our mind, will, or emotions, but by our 'inner' true selves, born of God. Many Christians use their soulish responses to attempt to discern the things of God and it is impossible to do so.

*The natural, non-spiritual man does not accept or welcome or admit into his heart the gifts and teachings and revelations of the Spirit of God, for they are folly (meaningless nonsense) to him ... because they are spiritually discerned.*          (1 Corinthians 2:14 AMP)

This scripture is not just talking about non-redeemed man, but also the unredeemed parts of ourselves, our 'old nature', which battles for control and which needs to be subject to our spirits.

### Character

'God speaks prophetically to enable us to enter into his divine nature. Careful attention to our character response will ensure that we are co-operating with the Holy Spirit to achieve this aim.'

(Graham Cooke)

A mystery about the operation of the gifts of the Spirit is that once released they are within our hands. The word says the gifts of the Lord are without reproach, which can mean that the prophetic gift can continue to be active even for those who have fallen into sin (see Romans 11:29).

We also see in part and prophesy in part and so even words from well-known 'prophets' need to be weighed and judged.

Our own character will play a part in fulfilment. Are we cynical, with hearts of unbelief?

While the gifts can still operate through us, we will one day be accountable for our words and our character can affect the interpretation and understanding of the message by others. While the Lord does not withdraw His gifts, our lives are for His glory and worship and so we must look at our character as givers and receivers of His word.

### What's the fruit?

Ephesians 5 gives great wisdom in how to live in the light. Ephesians 5:9 says that *'the fruit (the effect, the product) of the Light or the Spirit [consists]* *in every form of kindly goodness, uprightness of heart, and trueness of life'* (AMP).

Galatians 5:22 says *'the fruit of the Spirit is love, joy, peace...'* Fear has no place in the presence of God. The only fear we can have is a good fear – the fear of the Lord. If revelation leads people to fear wrongly then it is not coming from the Spirit of God.

Some revelation is neither from God nor the enemy – but from the spirit of man. Words can be given under pressure, to gain respect or maintain a reputation. They can have started in the Spirit but finished in the flesh. We need to discern revelation from man as well as from God.

### Wisdom

Revelation is best partnered with wisdom. Revelation without wisdom can lead to confusion and even division. We see in part ... we prophesy in part. Wisdom will understand this and administer the revelation *wisely!*

> *The wisdom from above is first of all pure (undefiled); then it is peace-loving, courteous (considerate, gentle). [It is willing to] yield to reason, full of compassion and good fruits; it is wholehearted and straightforward, impartial and unfeigned (free from doubts, wavering, and insincerity).* (James 3:17 AMP)

James gives good advice in looking for wisdom from above – not earthly wisdom but the wisdom which is *far above riches.*

### Faith

When we receive words which we discern to be good and accurate we then need to respond with faith. Without faith it is impossible to please God and when He speaks prophetically we must exercise faith and not harden our hearts in the waiting (see Hebrews 3:7–12).

## Weighing prophecy

'The true purpose of prophecy is to build up, admonish and stir up, encourage and release from pain and discomfort, and to enable people to know and understand the heartbeat of God for themselves. If it doesn't achieve that, it is not true prophecy.'

(Graham Cooke)

*Beloved, do not put faith in every spirit, but prove (test) the spirits to discover whether they proceed from God; for many false prophets have gone forth into the world. By this you may know (perceive and recognize) the Spirit of God: every spirit which acknowledges and confesses [the fact] that Jesus Christ (the Messiah) [actually] has become man and has come in the flesh is of God [has God for its source].* (1 John 4:1–2 AMP)

### The tests

- Does it edify, exhort and comfort (1 Corinthians 14:3)?
- Is it from the Spirit of God, of man or an evil spirit (1 John 4:1–2)?
- Does it conform to Scripture?
- Does it lead us to the feet of Jesus?
- Does it glorify Jesus (John 16:14)?
- Is it manipulative or controlling?

## Tending the ground

'God speaks prophetically to enable us to enter into his divine nature. Careful attention to our character response will ensure that we are cooperating with the Hoy Spirit to achieve this aim.'

(Graham Cooke)

Hebrews 3:7 challenges us not to harden our hearts when we hear the voice of God. Just as a consequence of hearing His voice results in faith, so the consequence of not hearing results in hardened hearts of unbelief. There's no neutral ground for the people of God and it's sad to meet Christians who, for whatever reason, have hardened their hearts and live miserable lives. We reap what we sow with the word of God.

The Parable of the Sower (see Matthew 13) is a simple, yet profound, picture of our lives as the word of God comes to us – like a 'seed'. This parable is not just about choosing to follow God; it applies to every word that the Lord brings into our lives. It is a perfect 'operating manual' to use in discerning what happens to the prophetic word and explains why many words are not fulfilled, for they are conditional upon the receiver having the right 'ground' to enable the word to grow, bear fruit and multiply.

The first seed didn't even land on soil. It missed and fell on a path. There was no place for it to grow.

I have a bag of seed in my office. A friend in Ireland gave it to me. It is Irish grass seed given to me to signify my inheritance and call to Ireland. It's been on my shelf for several years, yet no grass has ever grown from it. No one would expect it to grow in a bag on a shelf. It needs soil, water and protection. Yet I know many people who treat their prophetic words in exactly the same way. They put them on a shelf in their office, with a 'maybe' or 'wait and see' label on them. There is no response, not even a yes or no. Now I realise that some words do have a time attached and they need to be 'pending', but even this needs to be from a faith position, rather than a 'maybe'. They do not understanding the importance of their own role in receiving and engaging with God in the outworking of the word. We can't make the word happen, but we can position ourselves so our hearts and minds are prepared for when it does.

The second seed fell on rocky soil, springing up quickly but not taking root. These are people who eagerly receive prophetic words, but do not value them, quickly forgetting them in favour of the next 'thing'. It was not unusual, when we were first travelling in ministry, to be asked to minister at the end of a conference. There was an expectation that this meant we were to prophesy over any of the delegates who came up for prayer. One time we were still prophesying at 1 am when I recognised someone who had already been prayed for earlier in the evening. When I asked her why she had come back a second time she said she hadn't liked the first word and came back to get the word she wanted, not the one I'd given! Some people like to collect prophetic words from 'famous' ministries, placing more value on who had given the word than responding to God's intention for the word. This is dangerous practice and can lead to despising prophecy and probably, unwittingly, despising God by making the giver of the word a 'king' to us.

The third seed fell among thorns and was choked by worries, cares and deceitfulness of wealth. Some people can't receive words because there is so much else crowding in or they can't pay the price of fulfilment. Prophecy is a change agent, and when we receive a word we need to be prepared to change. Jesus said that no one builds a building without first counting the cost and the same is true of embracing a prophetic word. There will be a cost to us – maybe money, plans, ambition or anything that stands to choke the word. When this happens it is good to have a pastoral approach alongside the prophetic, to enable the word to be received, understood and valued.

The last seed fell on good soil and produced up to a hundredfold of fruit. This is such an encouragement and joy as we realise that even a single word has much more of God's purpose and power than we could imagine. He's doing so much more with that word than just giving it to one person. It has life and power attached and the consequences of the outworking of that work are countless.

For churches, ministries or organisations receiving words, which apply in the corporate context, we advise the following steps for leadership to take:

### Step 1: Test the word

- Test the word to see if it is from God (1 John 4:1)
- Wait for confirmation (2 Corinthians 13:1)
- Let peace be your umpire (Colossians 3:15)

### Step 2: Decide if you want to receive the word

- Consider what your life, church, family, situation etc. will look like if this word is fulfilled.
- What changes would need to take place? Practically and also in *you*!
- What character issues would need addressing if you receive this word?
- How will you have to adapt to allow the word to be planted in your life, church etc.?
- Take advice from wise counsellors so they can help you identify the cost/price.

### Step 3: Count the cost and decide if you are willing to pay the price

- What current plans will have to be changed, abandoned, delayed?
- What training or equipping will you/others need to prepare for the word?
- What cost, in time or money, will be needed?
- What prayer strategy will you need to pray through the steps to the fulfilment of the word?
- What will people think?
- Will you be misunderstood, rejected, replaced, criticised?

### Step 4: Identify a strategy and communicate the plan

- Communicate and submit to others who have a right to speak into the plan
- Set goals, timeframe, personnel (if appropriate) needed

- Plan the training and development needed
- Identify the people and resources connected to the plan
- Pray throughout all stages, being willing to adjust and adapt as the Lord leads

So you can see that, although the Lord may make His will and intention known to us, He allows us the right to respond to His will. He did the same to Adam, Moses, Mary, Jesus, and will do so to everyone who hears His word.

Hearing is never the key issue – responding is the issue. That's why so many of us keep our words in gilded cages, imprisoning them to suspension in time, yet robbing ourselves of the privilege and joy of being part of the eternal plan on earth. The Kingdom Plan.

# Releasing the Word

> 'The true purpose of prophecy is to build up, admonish and stir up, encourage and release from pain and discomfort, and to enable people to know and understand the heartbeat of God for themselves. If it doesn't achieve that, it is not true prophecy.'
>
> (Graham Cooke)

Prophecy comes with a purpose attached to it. There is power inside to explode the purpose into fulfilment. However, there is a constraint on that fulfilment which is the measure of faith that is applied when the word is received.

God has always spoken to His people. The words of His prophets are still valued today. Are they any use to us?

Hebrews 4:2 makes it clear that the gospel message had been revealed to them but did not benefit them because it was not mixed with *faith*.

God speaks in many ways and we need to understand how to interpret God's intention for the word He speaks over our lives. Each word has a specific purpose and if we mis-interpret the word we can end up confused, disappointed or disengaged.

We, as we reflect our Father and all that He is, also have a part of His creative nature, and redemption restores us to that ability to move in creative ways to release His word to the world.

The enemy has an ultimate objective on earth and that is to retain power on earth through control of people.

He hates the prophetic. It brings the revealed will of God to earth, with the inherent power for fulfilment of that will as people receive, believe and release the word by doing His will.

God's kingdom is where His will is done.

It is the outworking of the Father's will, revealed through His Word (Jesus), released by His Spirit and embraced by His children.

So revelation of His word is crucial to the operation of the kingdom on earth. All God's power, will and authority is manifest through His word.

That is why Jesus is the Word – He is speaking the Father's will.

So this word releases the will of God. Jesus said the word must be released and nothing can stop it.

When the Pharisees complained about the disciples prophesying Jesus told them that if He rebuked them, then the very stones would have to cry out (see Luke 19:39–41)!

Such is the power of the word of God that we carry in us!

## Prophecy in the church context

> 'The context of prophecy is always into the local church. The church is God's idea. A called out group of people who are brought together through the life, death and resurrection of the Lord Jesus Christ ... If the gift of prophecy and prophetic ministry is to take its rightful place in the local church, we must establish some ground rules.'
>
> (Graham Cooke)

There are different levels of gift and ministry operating in the church and there are different types of prophecy. This workbook focuses on the development of the gift of prophecy, which is the area in which the majority of prophetic people minister.

The three main areas of administration of the gift are:

- The gift of prophecy
- The prophetic ministry
- The office of the prophet

### The gift of prophecy

All believers are encouraged to eagerly desire and move in the gift of prophecy. So everyone can prophesy if they seek God for the gift. It is one of the gifts of the Spirit, which are distributed throughout the church by the Holy Spirit. Whereas the other gifts are given according to the will of the Holy Spirit, the gift of prophecy is the only one that Scripture says everyone can have (see 1 Corinthians 12:1–11).

### The prophetic ministry

Prophetic ministry may develop out of moving in the gift of prophecy but not everyone is called to a prophetic ministry. The prophetic gift may be strongly manifest, accurate and regular, but this does not equate to having a calling to the prophetic ministry as a main calling. It may be a secondary calling to support the main ministry, such as teaching, pastoral or evangelistic ministries.

It is important for people to realise that regular use of the gift does not assume a ministry. God's ways are not our ways and the church does not operate like the world, where we can expect to aspire to 'promotion' on the basis of our gifts.

### The office of a prophet

The prophet will have a strategic voice and position of authority to speak to churches cities, regions and nations.

Most prophecy in the church is inspirational; it speaks for the edification, exhortation and comfort to the people of God (1 Corinthians 14:3). The church is a place for equipping the people of God for works of service so it is important that we equip people to minister in the gift of prophecy with integrity and accountability.

Most Spirit-filled Christians would agree that the church is not a building but a relational and functional group of people, called out and called together to serve the Lord Jesus Christ.

Identifying a protocol for operation of the prophetic gift, along with the other gifts and every service, is not an establishment of a 'law' for a church that is founded on grace, but a practical response to the need for order, which is the scriptural commendation (1 Corinthians 14:40).

### Inspirational Prophecy

Inspirational prophecy will inspire people to receive the love of God, be encouraged to move deeper into Him and His purposes, release worship and prayer, provoke faith and build up the people of God.

As the people of God receive and move in spiritual gifts it is inevitable that they will pass through different stages of growth and development.

In order to encourage development of the gift, while being careful about the whole church context, it is advisable to provide guidelines in the administration of the gift, training opportunities to practise the gift and access to someone who can be a mentor or adviser to those seeking to grow in the gift.

A culture of accountability, with freedom and grace, is an ideal environment in which individuals can develop and grow.

Training and discipleship opportunities will provide a safe environment for that growth while allowing a measure of practise and teaching to motivate and encourage individuals.

Feedback on content, delivery, accuracy and attitude is invaluable in both general discipleship and in development of the gift.

### How God expresses Himself

- In His nature – who He is
- By His actions – what He does

- In what He says – the Living Word
- In the wonder and beauty of all creation

The Bible is full of creative expression of God through symbolism, parables and prophecies. Even the design of the temple was full of symbolic representation of God's purposes.

The Holy Spirit is continually revealing Christ to us through everything around us – music, art, nature, acts, events, etc.

Even language is merely a symbol to express meaning. Pictures (images) are evoked in the heart and we see through them. Interpretation can be added to bring greater meaning and purposes to the images.

We are not limited to our ability to express verbally in order to release prophetic words.

## Practical steps

Most operation of the gift of prophecy is at the level of encouragement. Words of encouragement are a blessing to those who receive them and we need to have hearts to encourage at all times.

Prophetic 'words' can be communicated in many different ways, usually verbally, but also by other means, such as drama, art, music, 'acts' which demonstrate God's heart.

Recording words given is invaluable as an accurate record of what is said. We recommend recording the words on tape or CD as the initial 'hearing' can be subjectively received. Later review of the words can reveal a wider context or meaning to the original interpretation. It is also helpful to have an accurate record to share with others, who can contribute to the interpretation or further encouragement.

Revelatory words needs weighing and judging (1 Corinthians 14:29). NB: *We judge the words not the giver!* They must line up with Scripture and need confirmation by two or three witnesses.

## Guidelines for directional prophecy

Prophecy with a directional or correctional aspect needs more specific protocol to ensure our hearts and actions are in line with the heart of God. The person giving the word is accountable and I advise the following:

### 1. Give the word in private first, not in public

We don't have to speak as soon as we receive a word – God is eternal and a God of order, so don't react or rush to give revelation. Revelatory prophecy has implications for the wider leadership, who are accountable for what is given to the congregation. We must respect and work with God-given leadership.

### 2. Record the prophecy

Written or taped recordings of the word can allow a wider group of people to hear and weigh the word, giving attention to detail which can be lost if the word is unrecorded and then re-interpreted. Isaiah 30:8 indicates the value of recording prophecy: '*Go now, write it on a tablet for them, inscribe it on a scroll, that for the days to come it may be an everlasting witness.*'

### 3. Allow the Lord to touch our hearts first

We need to search our own hearts before giving a word of direction or correction to the Body. We need to ensure that the source is pure and that we do not embellish or influence in line with our own opinions or prejudices.

### 4. Understand your own accountability

We need to have earned the right to speak revelatory words. The church has a governmental structure and prophecy fits within that structure, even if giving correctional words. The decision to act on the prophecy lies with the leadership and we must not seek to gain a following of support for ourselves or our words. Integrity and accountability are key characteristics which prophetic people should seek to develop.

# PART 3

## *Living the Word*

# A Lifestyle Response

> '*I have given them your word and the world has hated them, for they are not of the world any more than I am of the world. My prayer is not that you take them out of the world but that you protect them from the evil one. They are not of the world, even as I am not of it.*'
> (John 17:14–16)

> '*Let me tell you why you are here. You're here to be salt-seasoning that brings out the God-flavors of this earth . . .*
>
> *Here's another way to put it: You're here to be **light**, bringing out the God-colors in the **world**. God is not a secret to be kept. We're going public with this, as public as a city on a hill. If I make you **light**-bearers, you don't think I'm going to hide you under a bucket, do you? I'm putting you on a **light** stand. Now that I've put you there on a hilltop, on a **light** stand – shine! Keep open house; be generous with your lives. By opening up to others, you'll prompt people to open up with God, this generous Father in heaven.*'
> (Matthew 5:13–16 MSG, emphasis added)

Jesus had a lot of say about the 'world' and what we should be aware of as we live this life on earth – as we are 'in the world, but not of it'.

All these verses spoken by Jesus were not intended as 'nice words' to print on Bible texts or posters. They were our job description – to make a difference while we are here on planet earth. We are not meant to hide away from the world – we are just to make sure that while we're in the world, the world doesn't get in us!

We will make a difference just by being in the world – but we are also called to bring the Word into the world – communicating God's will through our words, actions and presence.

As we communicate for God on earth we will have impact beyond our understanding. We don't have to be 'religious' or 'flaky', but just in our normal contacts and conversations we can make a difference.

## A kingdom prophetic lifestyle

We are on a journey into our destiny. We have a destiny on earth as well as an eternal one. The choices we make in how we live our lives will signify who and what we have faith in. The children of Israel left Egypt for the promise of a life that was beyond their imagination and outside their experience. They started the journey in faith but the old lifestyle kept invading their vision. The challenge of living a life that speaks for God is that it is directly in contradiction to life in the world. When we become a Christian we really are a new creation. The problem is that the 'old man' is the one we are familiar with.

I didn't grow up in a Christian home, so it was a huge shock when I became a Christian to find out that many of the things from my old lifestyle were not compatible with Christian living. We lived in the East End of London and if a television or carpet was needed the usual thing to do was to find someone who sold 'off the back of a lorry' or get something 'knocked off'. As this was part of normal life to me it never occurred to me that these things were stolen. Words such as 'stealing' were not used, so it was only when I was married myself that I realised that most of the things in my family home were stolen!

I remember when we were first married and were furnishing our first home. I was working in an office that happened to be opposite a large carpet store. I worked on the fifth floor of an open plan building where the elevator opened straight onto the office area. One day the doors opened and two men walked out with a large roll of carpet under their arms. They were asking 'fifty quid' (£50), on the spot, to buy the carpet. They also had a van downstairs with a greater selection! Completely innocently I rang John up and asked him if we could buy this 'bargain' of a carpet. I didn't even think about it or realise there was anything wrong! I had left Egypt but there was still a lot of Egypt in me. There is a journey for each one of us – to leave behind what we were born into, to embark on the life-changing experience of the wilderness and then press through to enter the land of promise. The good news is that it's not whether we start the journey, it's about finishing in the right place.

We are influenced from birth with values, morals, preferences and prejudices and we need to learn to put off our old ways of thinking and reacting. Even those from a Christian home can have a mindset that is limited to a certain way of behaving.

## Following the cloud or following the crowd?

This is a key deciding factor whether we live a lifestyle that is set to conform to the established way of doing things or whether we hold the things of this world lightly, being flexible and alert to what God is doing and being willing to move as the cloud moves ahead of us.

A prophetic lifestyle is one that is constantly open to the Spirit of God, one that is willing to lay down the good things in order to enter God's best. It's a lifestyle that is very expensive in the world's terms.

**We are called as priests of the Lord – a kingdom of priests.**

## He wanted to be noticed

He clearly planned to be noticed, the young man with the brightly-coloured, tight-fitting clothes.

We were at a workshop in London, arranged for ex-teachers who wanted to train as freelance consultants. There were about thirty of us in the room and the young man recognised a captive audience when he saw one. For the whole morning he dominated the session, making funny jokes and sexual innuendos. He was loud, camp and lewd and he saw it as his role to entertain us, whether we wanted it or not.

We were there to learn how to coach educators in the UK, as part of their professional development. This session was meant to be a focused and serious time where we could pick up those soft skills of empathy, combined with an ability to guide others towards their identified goals.

I was not happy. This young man was taking over, wasting everyone's time and no one seemed to be willing to challenge him. By the end of the morning I was inwardly seething with frustration and entertaining unkind thoughts towards him and the trainer.

To be fair, it would have been pretty difficult to stop him. He was evidently skilled in his act and knew how to take control of a situation. How on earth did he manage to teach anything? What was his subject – clowning around?

The morning dragged on and I considered getting the train home at lunchtime. But the group was too small for me to slip away unnoticed and I did hope that we might at least learn something in the afternoon. Little did I realise that I was going to learn a lot!

The first session after lunch is known as the 'graveyard slot', where everyone is usually well fed and not inclined to pay much attention. So the trainer planned an activity in which we would work in pairs to practise coaching one another. We were to identify one or two key development issues for our partner to consider, drawing them out to focus on what they could do to achieve their goals.

I was happy that at least he couldn't carry on his act for this part of the session. I could escape his antics for an hour or so. I looked around to find a partner, but at 5ft 1in this was always a struggle. People were rushing around and pairing up but I was way below eye-level and unnoticed by everyone – except one. He was making a beeline towards me. Clearly I was his identified target and he bounded towards me with open arms.

For the next ten minutes I got the one on one version of his act. He minced, preened, performed and was camp in the extreme. It was almost unreal, except my reactions were only too real and I wanted to run away.

There I was, a Christian minister, having most un-Christian thoughts and reactions towards this young man. He was the last person I wanted to pair up with and he was now wasting the most important part of the day, talking about himself and making 'gay' jokes to me and anyone else within earshot.

In the Christian 'world' I was known as someone who taught people how to hear God speak. We had just finished a prophetic school where the last topic was about 'taking the prophetic into the world'. It went down very well and the feedback had been great. Pride comes before a fall!

Despite my strong, negative (sinful?) reactions I was beginning to feel the heat of conviction rising up. How could I be so unloving towards this young man? I quickly and silently prayed for grace as I listened to his stories of the many rejections and grievances he had experienced in his career so far.

At last he stopped talking, clearly wanting me to start the coaching activity on him. He hadn't asked me anything about myself for the whole time, although we were meant to be getting to know each other. He had talked about his teaching experiences, his poor treatment, his frustrations, and the unfairness of life in general, referencing everything to himself. Everyone and everything was relative to his own needs. He had what someone once called 'the disease of introspection' and it was painful to listen to.

Then he fell silent, looking at me expectantly, waiting for my feedback on his story. I was supposed to say what I had observed while he was speaking.

Well, that wouldn't be a good idea! If I'd said what I'd noticed he would be shocked. My thoughts were that he was a selfish and self-indulgent young man who needed to stop his incessant talking and obsession with self. I wanted to tell him if he would only stop demanding attention and listen to others he might actually learn something! After all, that *was* the truth, wasn't it?

I was feeling pretty uncomfortable, convicted of my attitude, yet not having anything positive to say. It was like a wave suddenly rolled over me and I realised that my harsh attitude and critical responses were the real issue here. I was meant to be good news and my thoughts were to put this man in his place, like so many others probably had done throughout his lifetime. He was a pain and most likely repeatedly rejected because of his behaviour.

Then, as I looked at him, I 'saw' he was covered in yellow post-it notes. These notes were filled with words and I sensed the words were not good.

He looked at me with eager anticipation and so I shared what I saw. This was a secular event and there was no way I was going to tell him this was a vision from God!

So I explained that I 'saw' him covered in post-it notes and that these words were negative words that had been spoken over him during his lifetime. These words had stopped him from becoming the real person he was made to be and they needed to be removed from his life. I then said that I would 'symbolically' lift these words off him so that he could be free from their effect on his life. For a few minutes I mimed lifting the words off him – occasionally saying, 'I'm lifting these negative words off you right now.' By the time I'd finished, tears were streaming down his face. He was silent at last and there was a look of relief on his face.

He said he didn't know what that was all about, but it felt great!

I realised that, for all my preaching about the prophetic, I hadn't anticipated the impact prophetic revelation could have in a secular context. God was breaking into this young man's life. He had something to say and something for me to do so that He could break in and impact the power of words over this man's life.

I must admit I was as surprised as he was. In the past I had planned my prophetic words. I asked the Lord for a word, He gave me one and I passed it on. That was the format I was familiar with and it worked! Now I realised that the Lord wanted me to always be open for a 'word in season'. He has something to say into everyone's life, not just the Christian's. Prophecy is for life, not just for the 'prophets'.

Prophecy is a normal, natural part of the Christian life. We are prophetic people. We are an expression of God on earth and our very lives communicate the grace and mercy of God.

Prophecy is not just for church, although it is crucial to build up and encourage the Body of Christ. Prophecy is God breaking in and communicating His plan and purpose – not just general, but specific plans that He has for individuals, groups, churches, cities, regions . . .

Here is the news. God has something to say and we can be His voice to our generation. We can all hear His voice and we can all do something with what we hear.

Jeremiah 29:11 is a favourite verse for many Christians. It can be found on fridge magnets, Bible markers or posters with pretty pictures of cats and often quoted as encouragement:

> *'For I know the plans I have for you,' declares the* LORD, *'plans to prosper you and not to harm you, plans to give you hope and a future.'*

Well, that's good to know. At least the Lord knows the plan and it's good. So I'll just rest in that confidence and be content.

But I think that the Lord has an expectation when we quote that verse. He expects that we will start asking Him questions. What *are* the plans, Lord? Show me the ones I need to know right now. What is it that will give me hope and a future? How will I know them when they come my way?

I believe that a crucial part of Christian life is to be continually pursuing those plans; continually seeking the Lord for His revelation about the part of the plan that is important to each time and season of our lives. Why wouldn't He want us to find out more about the plan? Is it His special secret that is hidden mysteriously in heaven? Is it just for us to find out when we get to heaven and meet Him face to face? Or is it specific, relevant, practical and timely for our life on this earth? If so, surely we need to passionately pursue revelation and understanding of these plans and how they apply to our lives, in all the times and seasons we walk through.

After all, God's will is revealed to us – individually and corporately. Kingdom living is about living under the authority of God and His will predominating. We live to know and do His will on earth . . . as it is in heaven. This is evidence that the kingdom is come – God's will being done. Too simple? No. The problem is finding out what His will is. Our flesh fights for control and we get confused about the will of God. We have the Holy Spirit to help us and the gifts that He gives. But we can misunderstand or misinterpret God's will. Prophetic revelation is only in part (1 Corinthians 3:19). We have Scripture to help us understand and interpret what we think God is saying. We have others in the Body who will also have their 'part' to add to ours and we need grace and willingness to see the bigger picture through other people's revelation.

## Immortal beings

'There are no ordinary people. You have never talked to a mere mortal in your life. Nations, cultures, arts, civilisations – these are mortal, and their life to us is as the life of a gnat. But it is to immortals, whom we joke with, work with, marry, snub and exploit – either immortal horrors or everlasting splendours.'

(C.S. Lewis, 1942, *The Weight of Glory*, p. 46)

What an awesome thought! Our physical bodies may die but our true selves go on for ever. For what can possibly destroy a divinely created being? The Lord Himself did not say he had 'killed' Satan, rather that He had overcome him and took back the authority, which was stolen. There is a final plan for all created beings – to live forever with their Creator or to live forever separate from Him.

But Jesus came for *all* and not just for the eternal plan, but also that we might live the abundant life on earth – as it is in heaven. We may just be passing through, but this part of our living has an amazing part in the purposes of God. You and I are in the plan. We were in it before the world began. Our part is significant and our words, lives, choices and decisions all can line up with the plan – or we can live our own 'plan'. Some of you will be saying, 'But I've missed so much, messed up, made wrong choices.' Rejoice, there's a plan for that part of our lives too. He is the Restorer . . . Repairer – and our testimony of failure is always matched by a great proclamation of God's ability to be the restorer of our souls, restorer of all things. It's true that it may not be in the way we would think or like, but His ways are not our ways – they are much, much higher. Shall we sin that grace may abound? What a ghastly thought! But when we sin, grace does abound even more. Let these words sink into your hearts, minds, wills, emotions . . . Receive them and the power that accompanies them. As you do, so faith will start to rise and grow in you and you will believe. It will be unto you according to your faith. If you have faith as a mustard seed . . .

## Time – the great gift

> 'What is time? If no one asks me, I know what it is. If I wish to explain it to him who asks me, I do not know.'
> (St Augustine, 354–430, *Confessions*)

In 2006 the *Oxford English Dictionary* identified the most used words in the English language. 'Time' came top of the list for nouns. This suggests an awareness of time as being significant in our awareness of its importance in life. Yet so much time in the twenty-first century appears to be spent on things which have little or no 'fruit', i.e. evidence of a positive outcome as a result of the time invested.

Time has more value than anything else on earth. It is God's currency for His plans and purposes for us on earth. Unlike God, time on earth has limit.

When we are looking forward to times ahead, it can seem that time goes by very slowly. Yet when we are actually enjoying the anticipated event, it flies by so quickly.

Other events can make time seem to stand still. For example, when a loved one dies and it seems impossible that the rest of the world can go on living normally. Death brings an awareness of time being temporal like nothing else can. We live as though we will never have an end to our days on earth, yet when someone dies we look back on the 'times' they spent on earth and realise how quickly time passes.

> *From one man he made every nation of men, that they should inhabit the whole earth; and he determined the times set for them and the exact places where they should live.*                    (Acts 17:26)

Every one of us has an ordained number of days to spend on earth. We also have the privilege and power to determine how we spend those days. Even if we seem to be 'trapped' in the events of life, we can still determine how we respond and read in that time.

### Wasting time

This is not about doing nothing, but not doing or living for that 'moment' as God planned for us. Resting is not wasting time, but rather honouring God in fulfilling His kind command to ensure we live in the goodness that rest brings.

### Redeeming time

It is possible in God to redeem missed opportunities and pray and minister restoration for lost years. We need to have an awareness of those things that are still open and available for our time on earth.

We will look more at time in Chapter 10: 'Knowing the Times and the Seasons'.

## Boundaries

### Moving within boundaries

> *The boundary lines have fallen for me in pleasant places;*
> *surely I have a delightful inheritance.*                (Psalm 16:6)

There is a responsibility for the people of God to know the times and seasons for their generation and to serve the purposes of God in them.

Boundaries delineate ownership, authority, responsibility and power. Most people are communal and territorial – identifying with a place and a people.

### What is the power of mankind on earth – individually and corporately?

It is the right and ability to choose. Our choices are revealed in our attitudes, responses, decisions or actions.

This is the wonderful power God has given us. It is the power that Adam and Eve used.

Our choices can change the world.

Yet with this power come responsibility, ownership and cost. Our choices are not just for ourselves as we are not alone on earth. Our lives impact those around us, as will our choices. Adam and Eve made a choice to breach the boundary.

### *Breaching the boundaries of God is inherent to fallen humankind*

Christians can sometimes fall into a trap of thinking that the freedom which Christ brings is licence to do whatever they want. Christianity requires a giving up of our own lives. Christ made it clear that we must also take up our own cross, choosing to die to self and pay the price of serving Him.

This is the paradox of Christian living – *we are free, yet we are slaves.*

We have authority to administer the power of God on earth. Our faith can move mountains. We pray and God hears.

Yet many will say that their faith moves nothing and prayer is unanswered.

There are many possible reasons for this and I suggest that one of them is to know the extent and limitations of the authority and power we move in. When we know this we can be confident in who we are and what we can do. If we breach these we are open to attack and deception. The enemy certainly knows the extent of our authority and that is the extent of Father God's specific will for us and the leading of the Holy Spirit in the outworking of that will.

We need both a revelation of God's will and a relationship with the Holy Spirit to know when to move in the time, the way and the path of His will in any given situation.

We can declare 'through Christ I can do all things', which is true, but that doesn't mean we can do what we like. There are boundaries on what we do. The Holy Spirit puts good boundaries around us so we move with Him, in the right time.

### *Jesus had boundaries: He only did what He saw the Father doing*

Jesus had all authority in heaven and earth. He told the disciples this and He also empowered them to go out and minister in His authority. But when Satan tried to get Him to use His authority by tempting Him in the desert He refused. He knew His authority and chose to use it only to do the will of His Father. Everything that Jesus did was predicated on knowing the Father's will and only doing what He saw the Father doing. He spent much time alone, praying to the Father.

### Boundaries are good, when they are God ordained

When the children of Israel crossed the Jordan and came into the land prepared for them, the Lord placed each tribe within a territorial area and declared boundaries around them. They were all one nation but each tribe had a distinct purpose and relationship to the other. Even their geographical placement was significant to God. It was important that they didn't even intermarry between tribes in order to maintain the distinction of function and purpose.

God's boundaries are for individuals, groups, churches, nations and generations. They denote our freedom and authority.

As we recognise our own boundaries and those of others we will walk in the divine order, valuing others and their contribution to us.

As we serve the Lord and are fruitful within the boundaries we have, He will extend our places of influence and authority.

Boundaries are also extremely significant on earth today. They are the cause of many wars and disputes. The enemy seeks to rob the people of God of their territory, natural and spiritual. He hates the church with a passion because where two or three are gathered, then God is in the very place they inhabit. The enemy wants to rob us of every place of authority and influence we have, as well as distract us from worship, praise and fellowship to prevent the presence of the Lord being manifest through His people on earth.

The enemy will provoke rebellion against authority and order in order to pull down the strongholds he knows the people of God have: strongholds of faith, love, unity, sacrifice, harmony and servanthood.

We must be more alert and aware of our field of influence, authority and ministry – not just in the church but also in every area of our lives. Our call is to serve in every area just as Jesus did – listening to the Father, doing what He is doing.

Life on earth in the twenty-first century is moving towards global, or at least international, control with consequent derecognising of national and geographical boundaries as having any significance in the political, economic or even social context. Within the EU nation-states are progressively less able to claim sovereignty over their own territory as increasingly higher 'powers' claim the right of intervention through legislation and the 'common good'. This means that nations, communities and cultures will find it increasingly difficult to preserve their own distinct identity.

## Types of boundaries
- *Social* – people identified by religion, ethnicity, occupation, class, lifestyle, accent etc. or those living within an area / community
- *Territorial* – marked physical areas on the earth – delineated by jurisdiction (political) or assigned wealth (property and right of ownership or use)
- *Spiritual* – supernatural power and authority to influence and establish the presence

## Paradoxical challenges
- The earth is the Lord's and everything in it (Psalm 24:1)
- The heavens belong to the Lord, but the earth he has given to man (Psalm 15:16)
- The Great Commission – go into all the world – no boundaries (Matthew 28:18–20)
- Only do what you see the Father doing – self-imposed boundaries (John 5:19)
- Love your neighbour as yourself – no boundary (Matthew 19:19)
- Forgive that you may be forgiven – boundary (Luke 11:4)
- The Creator is distinct from creation – boundary
- In Christ I can do all things – no boundary (Philippians 4:13)
- The body is a temple – boundary on behaviour (1 Corinthians 6:19)

- Consider the body as a living sacrifice (Romans 12:1)
- We are under a new law – the law of the spirit of life (Romans 8:2)

We are coming into a time when listening to the voice of the Lord will be imperative to living on earth, essential to understanding how to make choices and decisions in line with His will. Living a prophetic lifestyle will not be an option!

### God-planned boundaries

When the children of Israel entered the Promised Land they were given defined geographical areas for each tribe and these were specifically allocated to tribes in line with God's purposes. The prophetic promise of God given to Moses identified the extent of the land He had set apart for the children of Israel and, of course, this would have a boundary area.

### What does that mean for us today?

I believe the Lord is stirring us to be aware of the extent and limitations of our individual and corporate roles on earth today, in order that we might be ready to face the significant challenges, which are imminent within the global, natural and spiritual context of life on earth today.

Few can be unaware of the overt conflict against Christianity today in the Western world. Many Christians in third world, fascist and communist countries have given their lives for their faith. The Western context has been largely dominated by Christian culture, at least, and Christianity has been tolerated, if not ignored for most of the twentieth century.

The twenty-first century has seen a significant turn in the level of acceptance and tolerance for Christian values and also challenges within the church with the conflicting beliefs and values in areas such as women in ministry and sexual orientation.

The next phase – from 2008 onwards – will see the challenge to

Christianity impact every church in every nation. The truth will become blurred as humanistic values are debated and positioned within the church body. The middle ground will disappear and there will need to be clear choices made by individuals, leaders and 'congregations' about what they truly believe and the price they are willing to pay to testify those beliefs when challenged or threatened from within. There will be a type of 'civil war' coming to the church, with strong argument and opinion posed against the leading of the Holy Spirit. This will not be a flesh and blood war, but flesh and blood will fire the bullets and the church will be shaken to the core.

But this is a good shaking, one in which those who are clear about the truth, who allow the Holy Spirit to guide in every interpretation of that truth, are willing to die to self in order that the Lord can build His Church – not man. These are the days we are living in.

These are the times and seasons, great change and a new era for the Church on earth. Maybe the last era.

# Counting the Cost

> 'Is there anyone here who, planning to build a new house, doesn't first sit down and figure the cost so you'll know if you can complete it? If you only get the foundation laid and then run out of money, you're going to look pretty foolish. Everyone passing by will poke fun at you: "He started something he couldn't finish."'
>
> (Luke 14:28–30 MSG)

There is a paradox in living for Christ in that we can do nothing to earn His love, grace, mercy, blessings and salvation. They are all paid for in advance and we cannot earn them. They are priceless. Galatians 3 gives a strong rebuke to thinking that there is anything we can do to 'add' to the sacrifice of Christ, which gave us access to Himself, His kingdom and the power and authority that is integral to these.

Yet there is a high cost to receiving Christ. It will cost us everything – our very lives. My baptism verse was Galatians 2:20: *'I have been crucified with Christ and I no longer live, but Christ lives in me. The life I live in the body, I live by faith in the Son of God, who loved me and gave himself for me.'*

This is a mystery, we no longer live in our old lives but our new, Spirit-filled, lives are 'in' Christ and He is 'in' us. All He has is ours and the world has nothing to offer us. We are in the world but no longer part of its rule.

Revelation declares that we, called to be the overcomers on earth, are not to love our lives unto death:

> *'Salvation and power are established!*
> *Kingdom of our God, authority of his Messiah!*
> *The Accuser of our brothers and sisters thrown out,*
> *who accused them day and night before God.*
> *They defeated him through the blood of the Lamb*
> *and the bold word of their witness.*
> *They weren't in love with themselves;*
> *they were willing to die for Christ.'*

(Revelation 12:10–11 MSG)

While we are rightly shocked at the current revelations of Muslims willing and active to sign up as suicide bombers, Western Christians could be soberly challenged that there are people who are willing to die for something less than Christ, while we have the call to lay down our lives for Him daily. We also know that there are more Christians being martyred for their faith today than ever before. Statistics vary but a conservative estimate in 2001 by *World Christian Trends* in the William Carey Library, based on thirty years of research information, indicates a figure of 45 million martyrs in the twentieth century with a calculation that 690 people were evangelised per year per martyr (no direct causation implied).

We may not have to face martyrdom but we do need to realise that our lives are already given up in exchange for the new life in Christ.

Revelation 19:10 states that *'the testimony of Jesus is the spirit of prophecy'*. The word 'testimony' comes from the Greek word *marturia*, from which we get our word 'martyr'. In this context it refers to those who 'witness' on earth that the resurrected Christ is King and Lord. To be a Christian is to be a witness on earth for Him.

Our 'witness' is a prophetic statement of truth, faith and death to this world for life in Him.

So if the spirit of all prophecy is about being a witness for Christ, our very testimony calls for a willingness to stake our lives on that fact. When we give prophetic words that are from Christ Himself there is inevitably a price to pay – a death.

## The first death – giving the word

Usually the first death is to self. What will they think? Did I say it right? Have they received it? I *am* a prophet you know. Why don't they do something with the word I've given? My pastor/leader doesn't understand me.

## The second death – receiving the word

The next death is to unbelief and a choosing to believe God. God's word always requires a response. We have a choice to receive and believe, or not. Either way there will be a price to pay. If God speaks, surely we are crazy not to realise that He has the best plan for us. Our minds, wills and emotions will need to be taken captive in obedience to the Spirit of God in us.

## The third death – costing the word

In Chapter 5 we looked at counting the cost and paying the price. There is always a price in receiving a word from God.

Economists talk about the cost-benefit of any decision. Analysts can calculate a financial implication figure for a chosen course of action. We need to do the same with a prophetic word, which has life and eternal value, in terms of obedience to God and participation in His perfect plan.

A cost-benefit analysis takes the positive factors of a decision and identifies the benefits of taking that decision. Then it looks at all the negatives related to making that decision, including all the costs that are involved.

If you are struggling with a prophetic word, or wonder about previously unfulfilled words, you might consider carrying out a cost-benefit analysis on them and decide whether you are willing to make a positive faith response to the word. In our language we call that 'saying Amen' to the word!

# A Lifestyle of Blessed Rest

> *Therefore, since the promise of entering his rest still stands, let us be careful that none of you be found to have fallen short of it. For we also have had the gospel preached to us, just as they did; but the message they heard was of no value to them, because those who heard did not combine it with faith. Now we who have believed enter that rest.* (Hebrews 4:1–3)
>
> *For as long, then, as that promise of resting in him pulls us on to God's goal for us, we need to be careful that we're not disqualified. We received the same promises as those people in the wilderness, but the promises didn't do them a bit of good because they didn't receive the promises with faith. If we believe, though, we'll experience that state of resting. But not if we don't have faith.* (Hebrews 4:1–3 MSG)

We are free to choose how we live our lives. We can fill our time doing what we want. We can be busy doing good yet forget that He made *rest* an essential, integral, vital element of our lives – physical, emotional, spiritual rest is a lifestyle option for all believers.

Life is not all about doing – although doing is good.

## A command to feast!

God ordained times of rest and celebration so that His people could enjoy the life they were given. Western culture has lost the integral value to individuals, family and community that celebration brings. Celebration is an acknowledgement of the good in our lives. Leviticus provides extensive declarations of God's value for feasts. Feasts – times of eating, drinking and enjoyment. Even the 'Sabbath' days were to be holy feasts – in other words, a joy to experience, physically as well as spiritually. Our Western culture would separate the spiritual and sacred from the natural enjoyment of life. The Last Supper, celebrating the Feast of Passover, is the 'model' for Holy Communion taking Jesus' command that this 'feast' would be a reminder of His death until He comes back. He used the context of a celebration feast with His friends as a sign and symbol of who He was and what His purpose was. It was extremely symbolic, as the Feast of Passover was one of the most important feasts in the Jewish calendar, celebrating the release of the children of Israel from Egyptian slavery and the deliverance from every plague visited on the Egyptians in the land.

We have been released and delivered. We need to celebrate.

## Holy days of rest

God blessed the Sabbath. He called it 'good' and 'holy'.

We get our word 'holiday' from the word for Sabbath – 'holy day'.

Even God 'rested' – but He wasn't tired and He never sleeps! He let Himself enjoy His creation.

Rest is a permanent state of 'being' in God and also destination. We are called to live in the promised land of rest – the kingdom place on earth today – yet we are also on a journey towards our ultimate rest in Him.

Rest is part of our worship – letting Him be King – subjecting our wills and presenting our bodies. Sacrificing even our desire to be busy for Him, just to be with Him. We become still on the outside – and on the inside, positioning ourselves to let God be God to us – our King.

## Restlessness – a spirit of the age

God places such high importance and value on rest. We live in a restless world among possibly the most restless generation that ever lived. The spirit of the world provokes restlessness. Rest is the enemy of the spirit of this world. Restlessness robs us of our inheritance in Christ Jesus.

What does rest mean? It means *to cease*.

The seventh day was made holy because God rested (Genesis 2:24).

The Fall resulted in restlessness (Genesis 4:12). Separateness from God results in restlessness – of course it would! Rest brings us back into the presence of God.

Rest is good for our minds, our emotions, our bodies and our spirits.

In order to know the will of God our minds need to be transformed (Romans 12:2).

As we are still, we know Him as God (Psalm 46:10).

## The law of rest

In the Mosaic Law rest was a command not to work, indicating the holiness of the people of God, who were set apart for Him, trusting in Him, by choice. Rest is a sign of who we are and where we are with God.

We are called to spiritual, as well as physical, rest. God didn't have a physical body but He still rested. Why? Because it is in the very nature of God to be still, at peace and enjoying Himself, the Trinity and all that He had made. Being still – resting – is a sign of God and the people of God should emanate that in the world as well as in our lives. We should permeate the atmosphere around with the rest of God as we rest *in* God. God has the agenda for our lives, He has already ordained plans for us (Jeremiah 29:11). When we are resting we enable Him to speak to us, prepare us and enable us to be equipped to go out again and do those works that He has prepared for us in advance.

Even Jesus rested – many times. It was essential to Him personally and for Him to be able to do ministry. He lived in permanent rest, choosing to take Himself away to be alone with God. Even then the enemy tried to rob Him during this rest by tempting Him to do things to prove who He was. Isn't that just so for us today? Just as we settle down to rest we think of all the jobs that need doing, shopping lists, things we haven't done . . .

The enemy hates to see the people of God at rest. It's a dangerous time for him. As we rest in God we are open to His will, open to His word and allowing Him to come and be present to us. We are empowered in our rest. We are transformed in our rest, as our minds cease from turmoil and submit to the presence and power of God.

As we live in rest we are able to perceive what Father is doing – just like Jesus – and not succumb to pressure to perform or please people.

## The road most travelled

Time and time again the people of God went their own way and chose the 'human flesh' way of doing things, so God would speak and call them back to rest and restoration to the person, purpose and presence of God.

We love to dig our own wells (Jeremiah 2:13) and light our own fires (Isaiah 50:11) – and these two prophets were called to rebuke the people of God because of it.

> But now, all you who light fires
>    and provide yourselves with flaming torches,
> go, walk in the light of your fires
>    and of the torches you have set ablaze.
> This is what you shall receive from my hand:
>    You will lie down in torment.                    (Isaiah 50:11)

*'My people have committed two sins:*
*They have forsaken me,*
    *the spring of living water,*
*and have dug their own cisterns,*
        *broken cisterns that cannot hold water.'*     (Jeremiah 2:13)

It's now the same message for us today. This generation is busier than any other at any time. Rest is ordained from heaven and the people of God need to take note and choose rest.

Soaking sessions are taking off all over the world. Why? It's a prophetic response to the prophetic word of God – speaking to people's hearts and they are responding. It's about entering the rest – the presence and power of God – Emmanuel.

Hebrews 3:7–11 gives us reasons why the people of God didn't enter. They refused to listen and obey and hardened their hearts. God is calling us again *today* to prepare ourselves to enter that rest (see Hebrews 3:15–19).

Rest is a state of being in God: a sign and wonder to the world of the kingdom presence on earth through His people. The fruit of rest is faith – which comes by hearing (prophetic revelation of God's word/voice). When we are restless we are not positioned to hear His voice clearly. Other voices and distractions will win our attention and our faith will be challenged. God judges everything by faith – who we believe in and what we believe. Faith pleases God and releases us into our destiny. Unbelief leads to disobedience and so starts the vicious circle of unbelief, restlessness and disobedience.

Faith is always tested – the challenge is usually in choosing which voice to listen to – God, ours, or another?

## Taking the land of your inheritance

Our destiny – to enter the land of rest. It's a place and a person.

We are on the same symbolic journey as Moses. It's always the same journey out of our personal and corporate Egypt. We all have to cross the wilderness and face the challenges and choice of obedience, trust, faith and vision that the children of Israel had to face. Many may start the journey but reaching the destination depends as much on us as it does on God.

Moses was called to lead the people in. But he got angry and disobeyed God by striking the rock. Disobedience cost him the land. Sounds tough! Moses had taken the people out of Egypt and they had wandered for forty years in that half-way land – the land where there was manna – provision falling from heaven and their shoes never wore out. Manna tasted good at first, but the people soon got tired of it and some even wanted to go back to the slavery – for the food!

We can live, survive, in that half-way land, where provision falls from heaven and our needs are met. We can think it is the best we can get and even wonder if it wasn't actually better in the old life. We can wonder about that abundant life that Jesus talked about and not even realise that we are wandering around our own personal wilderness or maybe in a crowd, all on the same journey, with the same destination. But going round and round.

Entering the rest is symbolised in Joshua taking the Promised Land. He believed the 'promise' of God and this provoked faith in Him, overcoming fearing the giants. We will all have to face giants in order to enter our rest.

Joshua had to take Jericho – a symbol of the stronghold. The people had to do a 'stupid' thing – march round and blow trumpets. If they hadn't obeyed they wouldn't have inherited. Faith *enables* obedience.

We are called to enter, capture and inherit our 'land' – personal, corporate and 'on earth' places – so that God's kingdom is established (John 18:36).

This means that the promised land is not given, but taken. God has prepared it, but we must choose to enter it. Remember, God had delivered all the children of Israel out of Egypt, but only two of the original adults who left Egypt actually got to enter the land. The rest died in the wilderness, in unbelief. This was not God's will or plan for them. It was the consequence of their response to God's word, blessing and provision. They grumbled a lot, forgot what God had said and done and even when they got there their focus was on the giants rather than the blessing.

- It's a problem – grumbling.
- It's a problem – forgetting.
- It's a problem – not seeing the blessings.

## Assume the position!

It's all about positioning ourselves to enter the position of rest in God – being set apart – then He can move in and through us. As we respond first in our 'natural' obedience, then we will move into a spiritual state of rest (1 Corinthians 15:46). We can be so heavenly minded we misunderstand the value God places on our obedience in earthly, natural ways. The Sabbath law was given to the people *so that* they could be positioned naturally to receive the spiritual blessing, which would enable them to live the life God planned on earth.

As we rest in Him, we realise what is important to Him. Our 'rest' can impact and influence the people and places around us.

Faith in Jesus Christ is the only way to enter the rest. As we live in His rest so we abide in the Word and the kingdom of God is established on the earth.

So let us do all we can to enter that rest and see the kingdom come on earth as it is in heaven, for this is the true Kingdom Prophetic Lifestyle.

## A lifestyle of blessing!

Prophecy is a gift of the Holy Spirit, given as He chooses. However, there is an awesomely powerful spoken ministry that can impact beyond anything. There has been much written on this subject. Derek Prince's book *Blessing or Curse* is an excellent study on the subject. Derek notes that the words related to blessing occur 430 times in the Bible but words on cursing occur only 160 times.

Blessing is essential to life on earth. We are blessed with the gift of life and we have the power to bless others. Yes, we really do carry that power to release blessing on others.

If we sense that we, or others, are under the influence of a curse then we have the confidence of Scripture which tells us that Christ became a curse for us so that God's blessing of Abraham might be released to us. The exchange on the cross meant that Jesus, Himself, took all the evil due to us and gave us His blessing in its place. This is the essence of Christ's sacrifice.

Our faith position is that:

- We are *blessed people* when we receive Christ
- We can *bless God* with our faith, words and deeds
- We are called to *be a blessing* to others
- We can *release blessing* to others

Blessings come from heaven to earth and earth to heaven – as proclamations and declarations that have authority in the release of each word. The released words have accompanying power to effect the blessing. The words are outside of earthly time, space and circumstances.

## The first blessing

The first blessing was to Adam and Eve after God had created them (Genesis 1:28–31) The blessing was:

- To be fruitful
- To reproduce
- To subdue and have authority on the earth
- To have rule over every living thing
- To have food from the earth

## God ordained blessing

God even blesses *days*. He blessed the Sabbath/seventh day – calling it holy (Genesis 2:3). He blesses other days to be set aside as times of feasting and remembrance. Days are divinely ordained – every one and every one has a purpose on earth – for individuals, nations, generations.

He blesses us with *peace* (Psalm 29:1).

So what is a blessing? *Webster's Dictionary* cites 'conferring of prosperity, happiness and recognition on a person'. The *Oxford English Dictionary* refers to 'making something sacred – hallowing'.

A blessing is certainly an *expression and communication of goodness* towards another person, land, inheritance, nation or generation.

God blesses and, because man/woman have been given delegated authority from God for what happens on earth, mankind also has the power and authority to bless and curse. Those blessings have power attached to them. Words have power and blessings have significant power – beyond space and time – as they are imbued with the spiritual authority from the beginning of time.

In Old Testament times blessing was closely related to inheritance – passing down to the next, and consequent, generations. Blessing indicates love, acceptance and generosity towards a person.

The Hebrew for blessing (*baw-rahk*) means 'to kneel'.

## Consequences of blessing

### It can be passed on

Abram was blessed because he heard and obeyed God and that blessing was one which would last for ever – to all his generations and all nations. That blessing was infinite and inclusive for all (see Genesis 12:2–3).

### Others can catch a blessing from the blessed

When we bless those who are blessed – we receive a blessing, but God curses those who curse the blessed (Genesis 12:3)!

## Blessing impacts every area of our lives

Just as Adam and Eve were blessed relationally, with fruitfulness, authority, rule, food and all provision, so those consequences of blessing are the same for all God's children.

## Some blessings are irrevocable

Even though Jacob tricked his father into giving him the firstborn's blessing there was no way Isaac could take back the words. There was a clear understanding of the power of blessing and cursing and the reality of their impact on their lives. Jacob was, by his sinful action, actually receiving the blessing of Abraham because this blessing was irrevocable. Jacob was aware of the curse that would accompany the deception, so his mother declared that the curse should come upon her instead (see Genesis 27).

## The 'if' blessings

There are unconditional and conditional blessings.

The children of Israel in the wilderness experienced the *unconditional* blessing (see Exodus 16 and Deuteronomy 8):

- They had manna from heaven
- Their clothes didn't wear out
- Their feet did not blister from walking

And there was opportunity to appropriate a *conditional* blessing:

Conditional blessings depend upon hearing and obeying God – the law was an expression or signpost to enable obedience, but obedience comes from a heart that recognises, reveres and worships God by doing what He says and believing who He is – that He loves and cares and provides for His children. Disobedience is a sign that we do not believe or trust in God.

So the conditional blessings are many. Some were:

- The blessing of God taking on our enemies for us

*'Behold, I am going to send an angel before you to guard you along the way and to bring you into the place which I have prepared. Be on your guard before him and obey his voice; do not be rebellious toward him, for he will not pardon your transgression, since My name is in him. But if you truly obey his voice and do all that I say, then I will be an enemy to your enemies and an adversary to your adversaries. For My angel will go before you and bring you in to the land of the Amorites, the Hittites, the Perizzites, the Canaanites, the Hivites and the Jebusites; and I will completely destroy them.'* (Exodus 23:20–23 NASB)

- Blessing on our food and drink

  *'You shall serve the* LORD *your God, and He will bless your bread and your water.'* (Exodus 23:25 NASB)

- Removing sickness, barrenness and ensuring full lifespan

  *'I will remove sickness from your midst. There shall be no one miscarrying or barren in your land; I will fulfill the number of your days.'* (Exodus 23:25–26 NASB)

While these blessings are open to us today you will see that the conditions are quite specific: serving the Lord, listening to Him and obeying what He says. The promised blessings are given corporately and so there is a requirement for a corporate response. It is sad, but true, that those who broke the conditions of blessing brought trouble on their tribes or nation. This is a sign to us today that we need to be aware of our need for corporate obedience as well as individually making sure our hearts and lives line up with God's will for us.

There has always been an imperative to desire unity in the Body of Christ. However, this is not always a priority in the reality of outworking church life on earth. The flesh favours ambition, personal preferences and desire to have signs of success. This works against the challenge of unity and preferring of one another. I sense we are coming to a time where it will be the deciding issue in determining the blessing of God on regions, nations and generations on earth today. We cannot afford to ignore Jesus' last prayer.

While we are blessed of God as people who hear and obey His voice we receive all these blessings – but they *are* conditional upon being people who hear. They are the 'if' blessings.

### Deuteronomy 28

> And it shall come to pass, *if* thou shalt hearken diligently unto the voice of the LORD thy God, to observe and to do all his commandments which I command thee this day, that the LORD thy God will set thee on high above all nations of the earth:
>
> And all these blessings shall come on thee, and overtake thee, *if* thou shalt hearken unto the voice of the LORD thy God.
>
> Blessed shalt thou be in the city, and blessed shalt thou be in the field [**in other words, wherever we go**].
>
> Blessed shall be the fruit of thy body, and the fruit of thy ground, and the fruit of thy cattle, the increase of thy kine, and the flocks of thy sheep [**in other words, all our children, crops, possessions, fruit of our hands**].
>
> Blessed shall be thy basket and thy store [**never to go hungry**].
>
> Blessed shalt thou be when thou comest in, and blessed shalt thou be when thou goest out [**travelling and safety**].
>
> The LORD shall cause thine enemies that rise up against thee to be smitten before thy face: they shall come out against thee one way, and flee before thee seven ways [**protection**].
>
> The LORD shall command the blessing upon thee in thy storehouses, and in all that thou settest thine hand unto; and he shall bless thee in the land which the LORD thy God giveth thee.
>
> The LORD shall establish thee an holy people unto himself, as he

*hath sworn unto thee, if thou shalt keep the commandments of the* Lord *thy God, and walk in his ways.*

*And all people of the earth shall see that thou art called by the name of the* Lord*; and they shall be afraid of thee.*

*And the* Lord *shall make thee plenteous in goods, in the fruit of thy body, and in the fruit of thy cattle, and in the fruit of thy ground, in the land which the* Lord *sware unto thy fathers to give thee.*

*The* Lord *shall open unto thee his good treasure, the heaven to give the rain unto thy land in his season, and to bless all the work of thine hand: and thou shalt lend unto many nations, and thou shalt not borrow* [**debt free!**].

*And the* Lord *shall make thee the head, and not the tail; and thou shalt be above only, and thou shalt not be beneath; if that thou hearken unto the commandments of the* Lord *thy God, which I command thee this day, to observe and to do them* [**not oppressed or suppressed**]:

*And thou shalt not go aside from any of the words which I command thee this day, to the right hand, or to the left, to go after other gods to serve them.*

(KJV, emphasis and comments added)

### Blessing is a choice!

What a perfect manifestation of God's power working through us as we choose to bless one another and release words which have impact even beyond our generation.

When God gave Moses the law he made it clear that there were opportunities for blessing or cursing, depending on how the people chose to respond to His direction.

*I call heaven and earth to record this day against you, that I have set before you life and death, blessing and cursing: therefore choose life, that both thou and thy seed may live.*

(Deuteronomy 30:19 KJV)

There are ways we can actively bring blessing down upon ourselves:

- We are blessed *when we consider the weak* (Psalm 41:1)
- We are blessed *when we trust* (Psalm 84:12)
- We are blessed *when we fear the Lord* – a rarity on earth today (Psalm 112:1)
- We are blessed *when we listen* (Proverbs 8:34)
- We are blessed *when we wait* (Proverbs 8:38)
- We are blessed *when we act justly and righteously* (Isaiah 5:61–62)

God loves to bless – it is an inherent element of who He is.

As we are made in His image – carrying that 'ancient anointing' – we are a blessing on earth. When we release blessing it is more powerful than we can imagine. It transcends time, space and matter. It is released. Who can stand against the blessing of God?

He lays before us the power to bless or curse – the opportunity and privilege to release life and goodness into people's lives, families, communities, cities, nations and generations.

We have enough blessing to give away for we are blessed with every spiritual blessing – we lack nothing.

Ephesians 1:2–4 shows that God planned *for all* His children to be blessed as He prepared every spiritual blessing as He chose us even before the world was created. He *planned* our blessing from before the earth was made.

***Ask yourself a question***: In what way am I blessed right now – spiritually, physically, relationally, financially, practically, emotionally, mentally . . . ?

Abraham was blessed and his blessing carries on down the generations. God told Abraham that through his descendants all nations on earth would be blessed (see Genesis 22:15–18).

Abraham's blessing is your inheritance today.

# Knowing the Time and Season

> *Men of Issachar, who understood the times and knew what Israel should do.* (1 Chronicles 12:32)
>
> *To every thing there is a season, and a time to every purpose under the heaven.* (Ecclesiastes 3:1 KJV)
>
> *When the Son of Man comes, will He find [persistence in] faith on the earth?* (Luke 18:8 AMP)

The Sons of Issachar were known as those who knew the times and seasons and what the right response should be. In other words, they had wisdom as well as revelation.

Revelation is not enough. We need to know what to do with the words we receive and where they fit in the time-line of God's plan for our times and seasons on earth.

Wisdom is knowing what to do with the knowledge we have. The world values knowledge, for knowledge is in man's domain. Wisdom comes from God's divine intervention, telling us how to handle the knowledge we have and exposing human error. As we co-work with God we return to the original plan in the Garden. The world's wisdom is foolishness to God.

I love the verses in *The Message* which describe what God thinks about human 'wisdom':

*Don't think that you can be wise merely by being up-to-date with
the times. Be God's fool – that's the path to true wisdom. What the
world calls smart, God calls stupid. It's written in Scripture,*
  *He exposes the chicanery of the chic.*
  *The Master sees through the smoke screens*
    *of the know-it-alls.*                    (1 Corinthians 3:19–20)

## The groaning creation

All God's creation on earth is longing for us to live and reveal what
Christ has done (Romans 8:19). Imagine! The source of all creation
is in Christ. It recognises Him in us as we speak, live and move in
line with His purposes. All creation is waiting for something to
happen – for the children of God to be seen.

Everything made is made by Him. It is His. It belongs to Him.

As we live on earth we present the sense, the fragrance, the
presence of God to earth. Imagine! There is a response in creation to
the children of God.

That means everything He has created, including every human
being on earth, is waiting. Deep in the 'spiritual genetic code' of
every person is the ability to recognise and respond to God. God has
made everything beautiful *in its time* and He has planted eternity *in
our hearts* (Ecclesiastes 3:11).

## Moving with the times

Jesus knew His times, especially when the time had come for Him
to be revealed in power. When His mother asked Him to do
something about the lack of wine He rebuked her, saying His time
had not yet come (John 7:6). However, He honoured her by
responding as God required a son to honour his mother and carried
out her request. Neither could anyone harm Him until the ordained
time had come for Him to be 'revealed' (John 8:20). Even the
demons knew they still had their own 'time' when Jesus confronted
them (Matthew 8:29).

We are not to know the precise dates and times of the Lord's coming but we are to know the times and seasons we live in.

We have a friend who is in his fifties. He's just become a grandfather but refuses to be called a granddad as he feels he is too young for the name! He is stuck in yesterday's season, imaging himself to be a young man, resisting the blessings that God has for the new season of his life. What a tragedy! Even though I'm sure he loves his grandson, his heart is resisting, even rejecting, the truth of the time he is at and this will rob him of the joy of being who and what he is called to be to his grandchild.

Most of us struggle with the change of new seasons and it is natural to experience a measure of sadness for their passing. But this should be matched with a realisation and recognition of the blessings and purposes of God for the new season. As I write this our youngest son has just left home making us 'empty nesters'. It is a very strange feeling after thirty years of bringing up three sons, having all the joys and challenges that are part of parenthood – all the noise, smells, mess, music, friends, fashions, blessings and challenges.

Now there is no thumping bass music coming through the ceiling, no messy kitchen in the morning, no friends appearing at all hours, no evidence of others living in the house.

It's a quiet, strange, sad time, evoking memories and a realisation that there is no going back, that life has moved on and nothing we can do can stop it.

Where did those thirty years go? When did we become grown up? What do we do now?

While there is still the sadness of loss, I have a deep sense of excitement in finding out the purposes of God for this season. I don't want to hold on to the grief of leaving the old season, robbing myself of the joy of the new and the good memories of the past.

I want to have fresh vision for the new season. When we have vision it will impact our choices and decisions for they will line up with our vision. Without vision we can become random or self-indulgent in our decision making. When we have vision we can keep focused when things get difficult.

God has ordained provision for each time and season – spiritual, physical, practical, relational provision – He has blessings specific to the time and season we are in.

## Vision – prophetic perspective

We all need a personal vision, a purpose for living. We need vision when we are young to have a clear focus and purpose – to keep on track and not get diverted.

When we know what our vision is we make room for it in our life, planning and preparing for it in faith.

We need others to help clarify our vision to encourage and affirm us, to speak blessing, affirmation and release so that the vision can become substance. We often underestimate the significance and importance of 'blessing' and releasing one another and need to seek every opportunity to carry out this priestly function. We also need to speak blessing and life to our churches, that they will fulfil their corporate destiny.

We all have a pre-ordained plan and purpose and are called to bear fruit (John 15:16). God prepared good works for us to do (Ephesians 2:10).

Our job is to find out what the plan is and do it!

## Knowing your time and season
(Ecclesiastes 3:1; 1 Chronicles 12:32)

In this season of your life what is the Lord leading you out of so that you can be ready for the new? It can be tempting to stay in yesterday's season because it is a good place, a place of God's fulfilled word. But we are to move in line with God's purposes.

Consider what you need to review so that you can move

on in freedom, leaving behind what needs to be released (see Philippians 3:13):

- things that take your time but rob you of what God has for you
- emotional attachments which were seasonal
- people attachments which are not appropriate
- fulfilled dreams and visions of yesterday

## Understanding your current gifting and calling
(1 Corinthians 12:11)

While the Holy Spirit generously gives gifts *as He chooses*, there will be different phases of operation of the gift, new gifts and fresh callings that we need to be aware of. We must not get stuck hoping for yesterday's anointing if the Lord is taking us into something new. Some callings are very practical and integral to other people's ability to operate in their own gifting, e.g. the gift of helps and administration can be the key to releasing other ministries. All gifts given by the Holy Spirit are spiritual gifts.

What do you *know* is your area of gifting and calling today? Many people miss the joy of moving in the current calling because they are always straining for 'more than' is in front of them. This can mean they miss the very thing that God wants to do with them today and, maybe, robbing them of the very thing they are hoping for.

## Clues to identifying your current gifting

- What are you recognised as being good at?
- What kind of things are you asked to do because you can be relied on to do them well?
- What do you enjoy doing?

Even making tea and inviting neighbours in can be a ministry. It could certainly incorporate elements of pastoral care, evangelism, prophecy and even teaching.

For example:

A new neighbour moves in next door and you invite them in for tea and cakes – *you are showing the gift of hospitality.*

They share some concerns with you and you take them to heart, planning to pray for them – *you are showing the gift of compassion and the ministry of intercession.*

As you pray for them you receive a word for them – *you have the opportunity to move in the gift of prophecy.*

As you share the word with them, you take the opportunity to tell them about your relationship with God and how He loves to speak to His children – *you are moving in the gift of evangelism.*

We can miss genuine gifts and callings because we look for them to be more 'spiritual' or 'church based' ministries, with church 'labels' and recognition. Most of us spend the majority of time outside the formal church context and with non-Christians. God's heart is for us to be the light, salt and representation of Him in the world. We can miss great and powerful ministries because they aren't dressed up in the way we expect, or want, them to be.

### Know where you have favour – and you do! (Isaiah 61:2)

The blessing of God is to have favour – with Himself and with man. Just as Jesus only did what He saw the Father doing – so His obedience resulted in favour. Favour is a sign that the Lord is pleased with a person. We need to be people who can recognise and respond to the favour of God.

You will have people and places of favour in your life. They may be easy or hard places, but if they are places where you have favour then they are places to be for the time and season.

Consider where the Lord is giving you favour today (see Psalm 16:6):

- With whom?
- In what way?
- Which places or situations?

## Have a different spirit (Numbers 14:24)

As we set our hearts, minds and wills to follow the Lord, we will carry a different spirit into the world. We are people of promise and we carry that promise to others.

Caleb remembered what the Lord had done in the wilderness and he held on in faith and hope. The others, having seen and heard of the Lord's ways, did not listen or obey.

Our prime purpose is to find out God's will and do it! We need to fight dispiritedness and disappointment by spending time in the presence of God, becoming spiritually alert (Hebrews 4:12), being contrite and humble (Isaiah 57:15).

Consider your spiritual attitude today. Are you:

- Content in whatever circumstances you are in (Philippians 4:11)?
- Hopeful (Psalm 42:5)?
- Faithful? Remember, faith comes by listening, hearing and receiving the word of God (Romans 10:17; 11:20).

## Be discipled

Who has the Lord put around you to help you grow and change? Who do you allow to speak into your life, challenging and encouraging you, standing with you and supporting you? Do you let them? Do you plan and make time for this to happen? When they advise you, do you listen to them?

Make a list of those people who have influence in your life and ask the Lord about each one of them and what He wants their role to be in helping you be a disciple of Jesus.

Who are you serving today? Who are you praying for, giving practical help to, laying down your own agenda for, encouraging . . . (Luke 6:38)?

Be specific and write down who you are serving and also ask the Lord if there are new people for you to serve and if there are others who may need to be laid down for this season. If it's time to let go of someone then you will be releasing them into their divine time and season too!

## The lifestyle transfer

Our journey into a prophetic lifestyle is symbolically reflected in the journey of the children of Israel out of Egypt and into the Promised Land. I believe that the symbolism in this journey is a prophetic picture of how God is moving the church today. The changing face of life, culture and belief on earth has been a swift and radical one. Behind this change has been a movement in the spiritual realm that has challenged the advancement of the kingdom.

Christianity in Europe is now openly challenged and legislated against. Nearly every continent is facing conflict predicated around religious beliefs – with Christianity seen as a threat to be removed.

We also know that there are more Christians being martyred for their faith today than ever before. There are more Christians on the earth than ever before!

Through the changes in media communication we can now connect with one another across the globe. Christian TV and radio is broadcast to remote areas across the globe and we are able to 'gather together' in ways unimagined a century ago. The church can now relate globally in a way unimaginable fifty years ago.

The lifestyle God designed for us is beyond nation, culture, geography or social standing.

These are unprecedented times and the Lord is preparing us for a radical change in our own church structures and governments to accommodate the unity which He requires.

It is the same lifestyle He planned in the beginning.

It's a lifestyle that requires listening with wisdom, humility and understanding.

## The journey of life (Numbers 13–14; Joshua 5:13–6:27)

Just like the children of Israel we have been called out of the slavery of our old lives and have been taken through the wilderness years. The wilderness was not a place to settle, it was meant to be a short journey of transition in which the Lord would provide miraculously. Well, the Lord did provide, but it was one long journey.

The stages they went through are the stages we all go through in order to overcome the world and enter into the promise of God for our lives:

- *Egypt* – where we were
- *Wilderness* – our journey into God's promised land – moving from the old to the new
- *Giants* – things that would prevent us entering the land – we need to have faith to overcome and a vision for what is promised
- *Jordan* – where we enter the land – places we cross over in faith and vision
- *Jericho* – strongholds to take down
- *Canaan* – where we are meant to be

God initiated the call out of Egypt – He identified the people to play a key part.

The freedom came with miraculous signs – Pharaoh relented; the sea opened.

God provided new direction – with specific information, revelation and instruction – the Law.

There was divine provision during the wilderness years – manna, water, quails – enough to sustain 600,000 men, plus women and children.

Fire and cloud provided protection and guidance for the journey.

*But* an eleven-day journey took nearly forty years. The people weren't ready – still holding on to their Egypt mindsets, forgetful of what God had done and promised, grumbling. Then when they were on the edge of the promise they saw *giants* – and felt like grasshoppers. Instead of faith there was fear.

They weren't ready to enter the land because of their attitudes and responses to God. The wilderness was meant to be a time of getting ready to enter the land. They weren't meant to live there forever.

The last forty years in the church have been like the time of wilderness walking. Many of us have been privileged to see God move, giving new visions of a structure and lifestyle that is Spirit ordained and led. The inception of the charismatic movement started in the late sixties and had the hope of a church structure and government that would see the fivefold ministries and spiritual gifts flourish, and a key focus was on the call to prepare the church to be a Bride, ready for the Bridegroom to return.

It is not difficult to see the signs of the times and the move of the Spirit in the Church, as these are reflected in the popularity of books and songs. The Holy Spirit leads us into the new seasons in order that we might be spiritually prepared and positioned for the purposes of God.

The first few years of the twenty-first century have seen many expressions of a desire to spend time just resting in the presence of God. Some call this 'soaking', others are returning to the practice of Christian meditation. Whatever we call it there is evidently a desire to become more intimate with God, abandoning self and being open to whatever He wants to do in us. Many books have been written lately which focus on prayer and the challenges of living the life God wants for us.

## Worship – prophetic declarations

Worship songs written in different seasons give an indication of the heart of God for that time. Worship songwriters and leaders have a unique prophetic function in leading the church to proclaim their willingness to be abandoned to God's will.

As the Spirit inspires these prophetic songwriters so a prophetic message will emerge that will cause the church to respond corporately to the move of God for that time and season. As the words are released so a powerful proclamation is released, declaring a great agreement with the Spirit of God.

While some songs are timeless and stir our spirits to respond personally, many songs are specific to what the Spirit wants to release during a period.

For example, in the seventies there were many songs about being in unity, binding together, brotherly love. In the eighties the songs were of warfare and battle. In the nineties many songs emerged about the river, the King and the Bride.

While there are still significant differences between denominations and networks it is clear that during this forty-year period many churches have been through times of reviewing the traditional structure of church and sought to move in a greater reliance on the Holy Spirit and recognition of the ministry of all believers.

There is a sense of unprecedented shifting in the expectations of God's people on earth. There is a sense of imminent change and a need to get ready, to count the cost and be prepared for we are about to enter a new land, a promised land.

The prophetic ministry is now welcomed in many churches and denominations where it was rejected for generations. People are hungry to hear what God is saying to the people.

## Witness of faith

*He said to them: 'It is not for you to know the times or dates the Father has set by his own authority. But you will receive power when the Holy Spirit comes on you; and you will be my witnesses in Jerusalem, and in all Judea and Samaria, and to the ends of the earth.'* (Acts 1:7–8)

## What is a witness?

It's someone who reports what they have seen and other people are usually influenced as a result.

Witnesses are very important to God. They verify the truth of what He has said. We need to give a good report about what God has said. We cannot give a report based on what we think or feel, or we will distort and misrepresent Him.

We are to give a report – to prophesy – based on what God has said and we need to challenge, provoke, encourage and inspire others to believe because of what we do, based on what He has said.

A turning point of faith for the children of Israel came after the Lord had told Moses to send a leader from every tribe in order that they could go and see if what the Lord had said was, indeed, true. The Lord knew that the people needed a sign to provoke their faith during the wilderness years and He wanted the leaders to bring back their own report to provoke faith in the people. He wanted them to see that the prophetic word which had brought them out of Egypt was a true word and the evidence of their own eyes would encourage the people.

It didn't happen like that.

Each man went to scout out the land and they came back with their report. They didn't just look over the hills, they actually went into the land and brought back visible evidence of the fruitfulness which God had promised.

They carried that evidence in their own hands – indisputable evidence of the blessing of God. They brought back pomegranates, figs and grapes so heavy it took two men to carry them on a pole!

There was now no doubt that God's word was true.

However, when they returned to the people to give their 'report' they sowed seeds which would bring destruction.

What we report is very important to God. Our testimony can bring life or death.

While they could not deny the truth of what they had seen –

'surely [the land] *flows with milk and honey*' just as God said – their report was a negative one:

> They told Moses, We came to the land to which you sent us; surely it flows with milk and honey. This is its fruit. But the people who dwell there are strong, and the cities are fortified and very large; moreover, there we saw the sons of Anak [of great stature and courage]. Amalek dwells in the land of the South (the Negeb); the Hittite, the Jebusite, and the Amorite dwell in the hill country; and the Canaanite dwells by the sea and along by the side of the Jordan [River].
>
> Caleb quieted the people before Moses, and said, Let us go up at once and possess it; we are well able to conquer it.
>
> But his fellow scouts said, We are not able to go up against the people [of Canaan], for they are stronger than we are.
>
> So they brought the Israelites an evil report of the land which they had scouted out, saying, The land through which we went to spy it out is a land that devours its inhabitants. And all the people that we saw in it are men of great stature. There we saw the Nephilim [or giants], the sons of Anak, who come from the giants; and we were in our own sight as grasshoppers, and so we were in their sight.
>
> (Numbers 13:27–33 AMP)

All the leaders, except Joshua and Caleb, brought back an 'evil report'. It's not that what they saw wasn't true. From their human perspective it was all perfectly true.

The effect of that report was to create fear and discontent among the people.

God wanted them to bring back a word that would provoke faith, a word which encouraged, inspired and provoked them to take possession of the land.

Later on in Numbers 14 we find that all the men who brought back an evil report died of the plague. But Joshua and Caleb survived because they brought a word of faith.

Caleb's response was not to focus on the giants, but to move in and possess the land *as God had told them they should.*

His response was one of faith and obedience. He didn't deny the existence of the giants either, but he had faith that they were well able to conquer them.

We see that the report the scouts brought back had an impact on their life prospects!

The prophetic anointing calls us back to focus on what God has said, not what we see with our natural eyes, so that we can see with eyes of faith.

Absence of the prophetic leaves the focus on ourselves. Our 'natural man' has a vision – it's all about us running the show.

We are accountable for our:

- Vision and confession
- Courage and obedience

Faith comes when people hear the words God wants to say through us (Romans 10:17). Encouragement comes when people see that we live in line with what we say (James 1:22).

*Say what you see and we'll see what you believe.*

# Moving with the King

## All creation is waiting

> *Creation waits in eager expectation for the sons of God to be revealed.* (Romans 8:19)

There is a sense of imminent 'suddenlies' coming to us today. We do know that Jesus is coming back, that we are in the last days but we know we are *not* to know the exact time. We can, however, see that things on earth are moving very rapidly and that stirs the sense of urgency in us.

All creation is waiting for us to be revealed (Romans 8:19). While that's ultimately when Christ returns, we are also empowered and called to 'reveal' Christ today. That's why Jesus left, so that the Holy Spirit could come and work through us to see God's will and purposes fulfilled in and through His people on earth. What a privilege!

We are in a unique time on earth today and it's always been the case that the Lord speaks through His prophets on earth. Every child of God under the New Covenant can hear and speak prophetically. We can choose to ask the Holy Spirit to give us the gift of prophecy. But the challenge is in the choosing.

Our youngest son was an extremely lively and challenging child. He had a kind heart and gentle spirit, but he was often in trouble. He was used to having to face up to his misdemeanours and his strategy for avoiding confrontation was to slap his hands over his ears so he couldn't actually 'hear' what was being said. He thought if he didn't hear then he could avoid the consequences of his actions!

We're just like that. While most people are keen to receive prophetic words which they like, most of us are not so receptive to words which challenge or correct us. Prophets who bring words of warning or significant change are not the most welcome in pulpits or on platforms.

However, the Lord is speaking very clearly today and we need to decide if we want to be both hearers and doers of His will and not our own.

All creation is waiting for us to be and do what God wants on earth today. We are called to get the people on earth ready for what is coming. We have a John the Baptist anointing as part of our calling. The John the Baptist anointing was a call to godly repentance.

We need to embrace a willingness to search our hearts and attitudes to ensure that they reveal us as children of God, different and distinct from those in the world. We need to see repentance as a positive, redeeming part of our Christen lives. We need hearts prepared so that they can receive and retain the word as it comes to us.

Every Christian on earth is a prophetic voice for God if they choose to be. We do not know when Christ will come back but there is a call to us to be more *urgent* about getting ready for that. The children of Israel in the wilderness must have become very used to the way of life. The wilderness life must have been normal, especially for those who were born during the wilderness years.

## Letting go of normal

We may have become used to our Christian 'culture' and ways of doing church. It could be said that much of the ritual and formality of previous generations, which was superseded by the charismatic formats, is now found in our new ritual and forms of worship and ministry. We may have become complacent and consumerist about our expectations of church. We have forgotten that His ways are not our ways, nor His thoughts our thoughts (Isaiah 55:8).

Normal is a cultural expectation. Normal is modelled by those around us. We all like to think we are normal and it's everyone else who is weird!

As far as this world is concerned, we are meant to be peculiar (Deuteronomy 26:18; Titus 2:14; 1 Peter 2:9)! Peculiar is good. It means we are specially chosen people.

## Shaking everything that can be shaken

There have been many words over the past few years about the Lord coming to shake everything that can be shaken. It sounds like a good idea until it starts in our own lives.

Recently, as we travel in ministry, we have never heard so many stories of unprecedented shaking in people's lives. The shaking is among the leaders, individuals, churches, denominations and networks. For those reading this book I'm sure many of you are not where you planned to be five years ago. You are either not in the same church, job, home or relationships you thought you would be in five years ago. If you ask others you will usually find that there has also been a period of unexpected, significant change in people's lives.

We've come to the end of our ten-year goals, met our vision statements (or not!), changed goalposts, disbanded structures, moved through our projects and plans and have a sense that there's another plan just ahead but we can't quite see what it is yet.

Take heart. In the midst of the changes on earth, the Lord is above it all, shaking everything that can be shaken and positioning His people to be ready for what He wants to do now.

This shaking has been both internal and external – many people have described a physical, emotional and spiritual impact that this shaking has had on their lives. Many have been challenged to get back to basics of Christian faith and some have even had to take a step back for a season.

Much of the shaking has been in the church structures. We have all heard sad stories of leaders falling, leaving, dying, giving up … for many different reasons. Some of these have been the result of fallenness, but some have been the work of the Lord as He repositions us to be ready for the new age which is upon us.

## Getting ready to cross over

There's a wake-up call coming from heaven and we need to be ready to hear and respond to it.

The word that is coming to me is that there's a sense that we are leaving a forty-year period from when a new move of God came in the previous generation. This was in the mid to late 1960s, and it was a move which birthed the worldwide charismatic movement. We are at the end of this forty-year period and I believe we are about to move into something new and more radical than anything recorded in church history since the days of the early church. The world is a very different place today. The strategy for the church to fulfil the Great Commission will be relevant and significant to the global culture we live in and the Lord has a preordained strategy in line with His ordained timescale for these days.

This is the challenge we have today. Are we going to be those who continue wandering or are we willing to do what is necessary to enter the land?

Leadership will face the challenge of tension between the old and the new. The danger is when you carry yesterday's vision you can't see what is coming ahead. Church history is littered with stories of those who rejected the new move of the Spirit.

However, forty years ago national leaders were hearing and responding to God and their response ushered in a whole new season of the church being impacted and led by the Spirit of God.

## Promises of the land

Let us take encouragement from what God has promised. These promises are signs of His presence and power among the people (see Deuteronomy 7):

- Enemies will be driven out or into your hands
- Freedom from bondage (v. 8)
- Many children (v. 13)
- Prosperity of grain, wine, cattle, oil, flocks (v. 13)
- No barrenness (v. 14)
- No sickness (v. 15)
- No fear of men (v. 18)

It was a corporate promise – not individual. As we go together others will be blessed by our faith and actions. It was also conditional as the people were warned not to compromise or make any covenant with their enemies.

## Having a different spirit

We are called to be a Joshua generation – who actually can enter and lead others into the land.

The theme of Joshua has been picked up in recent years, mainly by young people who see Joshua as a role model for moving into the new place. Yet we must remember that Joshua was probably in his sixties by the time he entered the land and Caleb would have been in his eighties. There is a call on the older generation to take up the challenge of having the same kind of faith and vision to keep moving into the new. It is not time to leave it to the younger generation, for this is a corporate call and even one person negating his or her own call to press in will have an impact on all the others. It's too easy to have a disposability attitude which says the individual doesn't matter.

Joshua wholly followed the Lord. He was called by the Lord. He was commissioned and anointed to take up the leadership role.

His personal success was directly related to his attitude to God and the vision he held in his heart.

Jericho was a sign to provoke faith that the strongholds could be taken as the people trusted in God and did it 'His way' – even if it made no logical sense!

Before Joshua died he warned the people against idolatry and told the people to be wholehearted in their devotion to God.

Who are the enemies we face today? What is our Jericho and where are the giants?

Jericho is symbolic of a stronghold of man which stands as a challenge to hold people back from attempting to establish God's kingdom in place of man's.

This could be a picture of a form of 'church' which is controlled by the spirit of man instead of the Spirit of God. Jerichos are not taken by human methods of attack but by obedience to the word of God, acting on His word even if it seems illogical or ineffective in human thinking.

What are the potential enemies/giants we may need to overcome?

- *Unbelief* – in what God says is the true inheritance
- *Dissatisfaction* – lack of peace and acceptance in God's plan and purpose
- *Fear* – any fear of change or paying the price
- *Pride and competition* – believing it's all about us!
- *Worldly ways in the church* – Egypt thinking/compromise/mixture

We can take encouragement that when Joshua's spies did get into the enemy's camp they found out that the enemy was actually scared of them!

## Forty years of change

1966 was a significant year. What became known as the charismatic movement started and the Spirit of God started to move on individuals. In the UK there was beginning to be tension on the topic of ecumenism. In 1966 the Evangelical Alliance asked John Stott and Martyn Lloyd-Jones to address the opening session at their 1966 event. While Martyn Lloyd-Jones had been sceptical about the ecumenical movement, John Stott was more favourable and called for a reconfiguration of evangelicals into a new association. In 1967 there was an agreement to ecumenical engagement, which was endorsed in 1970 when the Alliance hosted a conference at which Anglicans committed to embrace this as doctrine.[1]

At the same time, in the 1960s, there was a remarkable move in the Catholic Church when a Council was called under Pope John XXXIII. The Catholic population across the world were asked to pray 'May there be a new Pentecost in our day' and the gifts of the Spirit came to be included in the document of Vatican II. In the United States of America, in February 1967, a group of faculty and students from Duquesne University, Pittsburgh, Pennsylvania, gathered for a weekend retreat. This weekend is often referred to as the 'Duquesne weekend' and is considered to be the beginning of the Charismatic Renewal in the Catholic Church. The retreat concentrated on the first four chapters of the Acts of the Apostles and there was an expectation that the Holy Spirit would make His presence felt. All present experienced a deep work of God within their spirits and charismatic gifts were manifested in the group.[2]

Through the issues raised at the 1996 debate a door was open for relationships across denominations, which enabled the inclusion of the emerging charismatic sector of the church.

When the Lord wants to bring in change, He raises up prophets. While John Stott would probably never call himself such, history would show that his conviction and courage in bringing his 'word' led to the purposes of God being established in the UK and significant governmental changes in His church.

The Pope, as leader of the largest Christian denomination in the world, endorsed a call to pray which perfectly aligned with God's purposes for the time and season.

So it's interesting to note that two men of God were willing to hear and respond to the word of God and as a result were significant in bringing in the new church movement, which was established on a return to church being led and empowered by the Holy Spirit. This renewal, unlike previous pockets of revival in different nations, led to changes across nations, especially through the Catholic Church.

There were three key themes which were reflected in both the Evangelical Alliance and the Catholic Charismatic renewal:

1. Letting the Holy Spirit have a place of prominence and leadership in the church on earth
2. A release of the gifts of the Spirit
3. Acceptance of the importance of ecumenical unity

These have always been the Lord's priority, but for generations they had largely been laid aside or embraced only in part.

They are still the Lord's priority in establishing the kingdom on earth.

## Signs of the times

At the same time as the Spirit of God was being released into the church, the Western world was being impacted by a significant change to society, culture and values. The New Age or 'Age of Aquarius' was being proclaimed and the contrast with what was happening in the church was striking. There was an unprecedented embracing of immorality and unrestrained indulgence termed in the media as 'free love'. Music, art and the media propagated these values, endorsing the 'spirituality' which was all-embracing and typified by the 'Californian dreaming' of the hippy movement, the Beatles' move from pop music to openly acknowledged drug-induced compositions. This has grown into almost worldwide acceptance of spiritual influences in all areas of life. Today there are few beauty salons which don't have some form of 'new age' therapy on offer. Things which would have been considered fanciful and ridiculous a generation ago are now marketed in the High Street.

We can be encouraged that pursuit of the spiritual can often make people open to the Spirit of God.

'Free love' became the cry of many youth and the mid-sixties saw a measure of acceptance of sex outside of marriage, the introduction of abortion laws and the increase in the number of children born outside of marriage.

The spirit of the world was impacting and reacting to the outpouring of the Holy Spirit on the earth.

What are the signs on earth today that reflect what is about to come? Jesus rebuked the people for reading the signs in the sky but not seeing the signs of fulfilled prophecy (Matthew 16:2–4). Many Jewish people were aware that a sinful generation would precede the coming of the Messiah. The signs of the times were everywhere to be seen.

Life on earth is shocking; in many nations there is either a moral breakdown, famine, flood, war, oppression or all of these.

These signs are a call to us to move in faith and seek the anointing of God to be a light, salt, yeast – an appropriate response to demonstrate the kingdom of God and represent Him in the midst of the darkness.

## Letting go

Much of the shaking over the past few years has been within church structures. Many significant leaders have died or left ministry. Many of these were leaders who were raised up for the new season in the 1960s and beyond. However, Joshua and Caleb held on to the Lord through all the wilderness years and were old men when they entered the land. Let us pray for the Lord to stir up the many who have the spirit of a Joshua or Calebs, that they will embrace that spirit and lay down the old in order to move into the promised land. Many of these are in their sixties and older and it is imperative that we speak words of life and courage to them that they do not settle for wilderness living or become those who have left it to the younger generation. All ages were to go into the land – not just the young!

There is a danger in carrying yesterday's vision and not recognising the time of change. This can lead to conflict and tension in the church. There's a need for leaving and cleaving of that which we gave our lives for ten, twenty, thirty-plus years ago in order to keep pressing on into the new.

We paid a high price to get where we are and something in us wants to stay where we are and make it work here. But God is saying that where we are isn't the destination. He didn't bring us out of Egypt to make the wilderness our goal. It was just a passing-through place. A place where we could get Egypt out of us.

The last forty years may have seemed like wilderness years as we look at the moral decline in Western society. We will certainly have experienced personal times of wilderness in our individual lives. If you are living through difficult or dry times remember the wilderness was a good place for people in transition. The Lord was with them. He sent the cloud by day and the fire by night to guide them. He provided water and food. Their shoes never wore out. They even had dinner flying in. All their needs were met and God was with them. Every day they had manna that tasted sweet at first, but became tedious after forty years. But manna was meant for an eleven-day journey and not a forty-year diet!

But they weren't happy. They grumbled.

Are we like that? We have never had so many Christian books, worship songs, conferences to go to, God TV . . .

All wonderful blessings of God. We need them and need to value them. But we need to be careful we don't think this is enough. We mustn't become consumers of the things of God, but need to be ready to move on and not be comfortable and secure in where we are.

There's a wake-up call and we need to be ready to hear and listen very closely to what the Spirit is saying. The Bible repeatedly exhorts those who have ears to hear. That means it's up to us to listen. That requires a stillness and a position to be able to hear.

## Knowing is never enough

We need to be like the Sons of Issachar (1 Chronicles 12:32) who knew the times and seasons and knew what Israel should do. It is never enough to know prophetically what God is saying. We have to know to do with what we know.

One of my favourite books is *Asterix and the Soothsayer*. It is an extremely good example of an ineffective gift of prophecy. The character, Prolix, travels from village to village giving prophecies for food and water. The problem comes when he goes to Asterix's village and they want to act on what he says. He didn't have a plan for that! In the story, of course, he is a false soothsayer, but there can be a tendency for genuine prophetic words to be 'sold short' – given, but not supplemented with an understanding of what to do with what is revealed.

It can be a source of amazement to me when individuals and even churches receive a prophetic word, get very excited about it, tell a lot of people about it, even print it out and circulate it for everyone to read. And then do nothing at all with it.

What is the point?

When we get a prophetic word we need to spend time pressing into God for wisdom to know what our response needs to be. A sign of believing God is living as though we believe what He says and preparing ourselves accordingly.

I have been given one particular verse as part of a prophecy several times now: *'Ask of me, and I will make the nations your inheritance, the ends of the earth your possession'* (Psalm 2:8).

There are clearly many possible applications of this verse in different contexts, but when it was given to me I received very clear understanding that *I had a responsibility to do something.* It wasn't just inevitable that the word would be fulfilled. It was a conditional word and if it was going to come true I would need to meet the conditions.

The first condition was that I needed to ask. I knew I needed to be more focused and serious about what I needed to be praying. So I have spent time praying and researching different countries in preparation for the specific places the Lord has for me.

It's not all about me making the choices, but it is about cooperating with the Lord and putting in the necessary preparation so I am ready when He speaks.

### Notes

1.  *Source*: Article published on the Evangelical Alliance's website: 'A Brief History of EA', www.eauk.org
2.  *Source*: www.ccr-ireland.org/history

# The Leadership Challenge

> *It was he who gave some to be apostles, some to be prophets, some to be evangelists, and some to be pastors and teachers, to prepare God's people for works of service, so that the body of Christ may be built up until we all reach unity in the faith and in the knowledge of the Son of God and become mature, attaining to the whole measure of the fullness of Christ.* (Ephesians 4:11–13)

Kingdom leaders are called and anointed by the Spirit of God, discerned and recognised by the people of God.

Leadership ordained by God is specific to the needs of the times and the people for each generation. Moses was a transition leader who could have become an establishment leader. His character lost him the opportunity to complete the leadership call to lead the people into the Promised Land. Joshua was a transfer leader. He had the spirit, the character, the anointing and a heart for the people. His passion was to ensure the people maintained their devotion to God and he renewed the covenant between God and Israel. This will be the mark of leadership for the new generation of leaders in the church.

All cultures and societies have forms of leadership. Original leadership was family based, leading to tribal leadership. Leadership in Israel was both tribal and functional. Each tribe had recognised elders who were expected to carry out a leadership role in both ensuring the people lived in accordance with God's laws and also carried out a government role. The strategic roles were held by prophets and priests. The priests were all from the tribe of Levi, so it was an inherited function. Moses and Aaron, as brothers, both carried the priestly function. Aaron was also called to be as a prophet for Moses (Exodus 7:1). He was the spokesperson for Moses and the 'voice' in the wilderness. It was Aaron who was used to demonstrate God's power when he threw down the staff that became the snake.

When the time came to leave the wilderness and cross over into the Promised Land there was a need for a different kind of leadership. Wilderness leadership was not appropriate any more. New leadership needed to have courage to face the obstacles, enemies and challenges and to take the people to establish a nation in a place they had never been before.

I believe the Lord is changing the face of leadership in His church on earth today. I believe that the kind of leadership seen in Joshua and Caleb is the leadership God is raising up to equip the church to move into the new challenges ahead. The Holy Spirit will inspire, prepare and reveal these leaders. Many have been hidden, some have been emerging over the past few years and some will be current leaders who will take up the challenge to lay down their old style of leadership to embrace the priestly and prophetic anointing. These leaders will have a different 'spirit' on them, able to hear God and move on the basis of what He has said and not what they see. They won't deny that there are giants in the land, but will believe and trust in God, inspiring the people with confidence that they are well able to enter the land.

There will be a 'changing of the guard' across the nations.

## Changing of the guard

In prayer at the start of 2007 the Lord brought the phrase *global government* to me. That same day I was reading the national newspapers and there was an article on 'world government'. I spent some days seeking the Lord for more wisdom and revelation on this and as a result I was aware of *four key issues* that the church will need to address in this new season in order to prepare the people of God for changes that are coming in the natural and spiritual realms. God has purpose for us in our generation and we are called to receive, reveal and release His governmental authority to outwork His purposes – whatever the cost! His people on earth are guardians of His truth and releasers of His will. Guarding is a key function for all of us. We guard our hearts to ensure they stay right. We guard our minds and take every thought captive to ensure they are in line with Christ's thoughts. We guard our bodies to keep them pure as a temple of the Holy Spirit. We guard our faith, standing firm in the face of personal and corporate attacks or temptations to pervert or discredit the truth of the gospel. I heard the phrase *changing of the guard*. I did not sense that this exclusively meant change of leadership personnel, although that was implied in part, but that the *guards* are being given new instructions and needed to be ready to change their position and strategy in line with these instructions.

Leadership has a key role in ensuring the corporate expression of Christ on earth, the church, is in line with God's plan and purpose for each time and season. Leaders guard the people from wolves and thieves. They guard the mission of the church and effect ways of equipping the people to carry out that mission. But, above all, they are to guard the Word of God – as revealed through Scripture and the Spirit of God. The Word and the Spirit together ensure wholeness and balance in the church. Smith Wigglesworth's prophecy from the 1950s spoke about the different decades when God would move His church forward. He spoke of a decade when there would be:

> ' . . . a coming together of those with an emphasis on the Word and those with an emphasis on the Spirit. When the Word and the Spirit come together, there will be the biggest movement

of the Holy Spirit that the nation, and indeed the world, has ever seen.

It will mark the beginning of a revival that will eclipse anything that has been witnessed within these shores, even the Wesleyan and the Welsh revivals of former years. The outpouring of God's Spirit will flow over from the UK to the mainland of Europe, and from there will begin a missionary move to the ends of the earth.'

This is encouraging to us today, as many sense that we are in, or about to enter, this particular time. However, there needs to be a realisation that this change will challenge both leaders and individuals in the church and will affect church structures, as choices need to be made on whether to embrace and adapt to what the Spirit is doing on the earth – or not.

I believe these four issues are ones that the Lord is looking to His Church to take up and seek His direction. They are issues that will impact the world, as well as the Church, and which have global, as well as local, implications for church government.

The issues will have impact in the natural and spiritual realms. They are issues for all humankind and will express and release God's purpose, from the time of creation, and in line with His specific purposes on the earth today.

## The issues

1. Global church
2. Gender
3. Apostolic government
4. Local priesthood

### 1. Global church

The world of the twenty-first century is a world beyond anything that previous generations could have imagined. National identity is being absorbed into pan-national or continental economic or governmental regions and alliances. European legislation has super-seded most of the legislation and control of its member states. Government on earth is positioned in the midst of rapid changes, supported by global communication technologies and transport infrastructures which facilitate global relationships.

The church is perfectly placed to embrace and exploit global developments in communications technology in order to impact unreached and isolated people groups through evangelism. Chris-tian TV broadcasting takes the gospel to the nations twenty-four hours a day. This brings the concept of community into a global context, as we can see hear and join others in worship, teaching and service through direct access into homes and churches across the globe.

Mission teams are now a normal part of many major Christian ministries, with ease of transport and relatively low-cost travel providing opportunities for individuals to go to the nations on short-term mission trips, while maintaining a home base.

The global context provides a unique opportunity for strategic, relational, global connections across national and denominational boundaries. There is now an opportunity for global leadership to emerge, enabling partnerships and relational connections which will serve the Lord's purpose on earth today.

A global church led by the Spirit of God could transform the earth through relational, servant-hearted sacrificial relationships 'speaking' to and across nations.

We truly are one nation – God's people on earth.

### 2. Gender

There is much concern within the church today around issues of sexuality, which threaten to undermine church government and leadership. While these issues need to be addressed, they are predicated on human sexuality being the critical dilemma.

However, while the church debates the validity of diverse views of sexuality, it seems to be overlooking more important issues relating to gender. God declared that man and woman – together – reflect God's image on earth. Man and woman were designed to stand alongside one another, upright and whole before God, imaging Him in their relationship and function.

C.S. Lewis in his book *Perelandra* said:

'Gender is a reality and a more fundamental reality than sex.'

I believe the issue of gender is one that will release or constrain the church in this new season. There is an urgent need to understand the masculine and feminine expression of God on earth in order to present a right image on earth.

God's love is expressed on earth through His people. Male and female qualities express love differently, but together they resonate a true expression of God. The church, in its male and female expression, speaks and ministers the heart of God. God is Father to us, yet He is not male or female by gender, for there is no male or female in heaven – all are one in Christ (Galatians 3:28).

The Father initiated love – as He first loved us. We are His Bride, a primarily feminine, responding role.

Yet males and females on earth express both masculine and feminine functions as initiators and worshippers. After all, the Lord told Adam and Eve to rule the earth – not just Adam. The earth is a place that requires initiative, action and dominion. Adam and Eve were also subject to the Father, made to relate to Him and respond to His will. In essence the divine plan for humankind is for people who are responsive (feminine) in order to initiate (masculine). Worship of God is the response of humankind to the Creator. It is a feminine 'response' and a critical element in our relationship with God.

If the church is being prepared to be the Bride of Christ – the ultimate feminine response, the issue of gender needs to be embraced, understood and addressed in the church on earth. Failure to address this issue will hinder the preparation of the Bride. The Bride is to make *herself* ready and all those who are part of the Bride need an understanding of the responsive nature inherent in both male and female.

### 3. Apostolic government

The call of the apostle was to be a servant:

> So then, let us [apostles] be looked upon as ministering servants of Christ and stewards (trustees) of the mysteries (the secret purposes) of God.                               (1 Corinthians 4:1 AMP)

Fivefold ministries are the functional roles necessary to build up the people of God, equipping them for their work, promoting and leading to unity, maturity and an increasing knowledge of God until we reach fullness in Him. Since Paul is clear about the purpose of these roles and the intended outcome of their ministries, we can look for these signs as fruit of the reality of that ministry. Is the result of apostolic leadership a greater unity, maturity and knowledge of God for the people? Is this their priority and passion? What's the fruit? We are recognised by our fruit. Or is their *only* fruit a successful ministry in terms of position, finance, numbers or profile? There will be a sorting and sifting to expose the root and fruit of what is established in the name of the Lord.

It was never God's plan for kings.

> It was he who gave some to be apostles, some to be prophets, some to be evangelists, and some to be pastors and teachers, to prepare God's people for works of service, **so that the body of Christ may be built up until we all reach unity in the faith and in the knowledge of the Son of God and become mature, attaining to the whole measure of the fullness of Christ.** (Ephesians 4:11–13, emphasis added)

It was God's plan that His people on earth value relationship above function, making unity a priority.

Spirit-led apostolic teams will develop relationally across the globe in this new season. Their values will be unity, relationship and preferring of one another, rather than building their own ministries. Apostolic functioning 'teams' will impact local, national and international gatherings and communities of 'church'. Apostolic teams will connect and inter-relate across the world, serving and releasing the people to preach, live and demonstrate the kingdom of God with signs and wonders following.

### 4. Local priesthood – local prophets

Another aspect of leadership, which will be significant in this new season, is the establishment of the kind of local leadership the Lord wanted for the people. The Lord had identified two types of spiritual leadership that He had ordained in the Old Testament context: the prophets and the priests. You will recall that it was because of the failure of Samuel to ensure the prophetic ministry was rightly prepared for the next generation that the people lost confidence in the prophetic function. When that happened they lost confidence that the prophets would be valid to speak on behalf of God. So they looked enviously at the world and took their model as their own. They made a king for themselves.

The Lord was rejected as King over them in favour of a king with flesh on.

> *'Now if you obey me fully and keep my covenant, then out of all nations you will be my treasured possession. Although the whole earth is mine, you will be for me a kingdom of priests and a holy nation.'*                                    (Exodus 19:5–6)

Every kingdom citizen is called to be both a priest and prophet. A priest without a prophetic spirit will not be able to proclaim and release the kingdom. A prophet without a priestly function will lack identification with the people. There is a call for team-working of prophets and priests and there will be many leaders working in tandem, across denominational and geographical boundaries, in this new season. Some will have both a priestly and prophetic anointing, some will be more 'specialist', but the new generation leader will recognise and discern those in the Body they need to be connecting with and they will seek to work collaboratively, honouring and preferring others rather than building their own kingdoms.

We all need both the priestly call and a prophetic anointing to live the kingdom on earth today. How can we minister the kingdom unless we are in conversation with the King?

How can we reach the people unless we have a servant heart towards them?

The new kind of leadership will ensure the people serve the true King and have kingdom values and strategies. Unity, humility, holiness, obedience and sacrifice will mark them out.

It's both an individual and corporate anointing.

Leadership of prophets and priests, significantly local leadership, will lead the people into the place prepared. They will proclaim, preach and release a priestly, prophetic nation to go out with the presence and power of God before them.

They will displace structures with strategies: strategies to equip and release the people to go into all the nations and establish kingdom rule. They will discern and embrace the truly apostolic and work in partnerships with the fivefold ministries.

Prophetic leaders and ministries face the challenge of finding ways to build relationally, for there will be a great value on relationship over function. Prophetic people will recognise and respond to the need to have a corporate voice, made up of many individual voices, rather than an emphasis on the individual. It's a time of personal sacrifice for the prophets and priests. Prophets will seek out others to connect with and share revelation. There will be companies of prophets gathered to humbly hear and release the word of God to the church.

I'm utterly convinced we are at the end of a significant period of church history, an end of the Holy Spirit doing one thing and a beginning of a new thing. There can only be one kingdom established and all other kingdoms must fall to the King.

> *'Moses my servant is dead. Now then, you and all these people, get ready to cross the Jordan River into the land I am about to give to them – to the Israelites. I will give you every place where you set your foot, as I promised Moses.'* (Joshua 1:2–3)

The new leadership will lead people to a renewed commitment to God. It is a call to holiness, separation and declaration, through equipping and releasing the people to extend the kingdom on earth. As the people are equipped so they will find that every place their foot treads will be theirs for the King.

God's kingdom on earth will be filled with prophets and priests for God. The kingdom will be established through sacrificial, servant leadership of the fivefold ministries. There will be global, international, national and local connections that will inter-relate and provide an infrastructure for the future challenges to the church on earth today.

This will be a season on the earth when it will be said in heaven that the Bride truly did begin to make herself ready.

> *At that time I commanded Joshua: 'You have seen with your own eyes all that the LORD your God has done to these two kings. The LORD will do the same to all the kingdoms over there where you are going. Do not be afraid of them; the LORD your God himself will fight for you.'* (Deuteronomy 3:21–22)

Another aspect of leadership which will be significant for the new land is the establishment of the earthly government the Lord wanted for the people. In Chapter 1 we looked at how the Lord had identified two types of spiritual leadership that He had ordained: the prophets and the priests. You will recall that it was because of the failure of Samuel to ensure the prophetic ministry was rightly prepared for the next generation that the people lost confidence in the prophetic function. When that happened they lost confidence that the prophets would be valid to speak on behalf of God. So they looked enviously at the world and took their model as their own. They made a king for themselves.

The Lord was rejected as King over them in favour of a king with flesh on.

> 'Now if you obey me fully and keep my covenant, then out of all nations you will be my treasured possession. Although the whole earth is mine, you will be for me a kingdom of priests and a holy nation.' (Exodus 19:5 – 6)

# Summary

> *Ask of Me, and I will give You*
> *The nations for Your inheritance,*
> *And the ends of the earth for Your possession.*     (Psalm 2:8)

There's a wake-up call coming from heaven and the church is rising in response. Heaven is rejoicing that there are many people who are ready, willing and able to cooperate with God. There have never been so many Christians on the earth as there are today. So many people across the globe are hearing and responding to God's call, declaring with their mouths and choosing to lay down their lives for Him. It was always meant to be this way. In times past there have been generations where the Spirit of God has moved on His people in small pockets of time or place. But today there is a worldwide company of God's people on earth ready to do His will.

It's time to get ready for the biggest change to government and structure in the church since the church was first established.

God's plan incorporates every one of His people on earth, regardless of nationality. We are all connected in Spirit and in the one great purpose of extending the kingdom of God.

Boundaries and divisions due to geography and culture are being swept away through the wave of global communications and media.

China, the world's most populous nation, has a potential broadcast audience of over one billion people. The kingdom can be preached in ways unimaginable from the early days of church.

The harvest is huge, ready and waiting for the kingdom to come. So let's have that Caleb spirit. Let's go out and possess the land.

**Let's be strong and courageous for we are well able to overcome!**

---

*For Christ did not send me to baptise, but to preach the gospel – not with words of human wisdom, lest the cross of Christ be emptied of its power. For the message of the cross is foolishness to those who are perishing, but to us who are being saved it is the power of God. For it is written:*

> *'I will destroy the wisdom of the wise;*
> *the intelligence of the intelligent I will frustrate.'*
>
> (1 Corinthians 1:17–19)

---

As we respond to the call of God to reveal and release His word on earth, we must make the cross central to all we are and all that we do.

Reformation is coming to the church in this era of twenty-first-century life on earth. This reformation will be through the evident fulfilment and evidence of Christ being formed in us and the will of the Father being established, through us, by the power of the Holy Spirit. This is more than an external appearance or an occasional manifestation of the power of God upon us. This will be seen in a shift of power away from human effort to outwork 'church' in the way we think is relevant to our culture and experience into a people with surrendered dependence on the Holy Spirit.

The cross will find a central place again in the church, which Christ builds on earth today. Each generation must find its response to the cross. It is the cross which enables us to abandon any belief that we can apply our human concepts to spiritual truths. The cross is foolishness to our human understanding. It challenges us to see the futility of our human effort and causes us to face the source of our desires, motivations and works. If we think we can do anything outside of Christ we deceive ourselves, for Christ Jesus came to do what we could not do. His sacrifice was to bring us the life He always planned for us. Our privilege is living that life is the power of the cross working in us and through us.

The lifestyle in the kingdom is one which allows Christ to live in us for His good pleasure, realising that He has already prepared all the works we are called to do. We don't have to find things to do, we have to find out what He wants to do – and do that!

> *My purpose is that they may be encouraged in heart and united in love, so that they may have the full riches of complete understanding, in order that they may know the mystery of God, namely, Christ, in whom are hidden all the treasures of wisdom and knowledge.* (Colossians 2:2–3)

The offence of the cross will be manifest in the church in this time. The cross always offends our human ways of thinking and acting. The message of the cross is a constant letter to us – a personal message speaking into our lives daily. It is a symbol of an eternal reality. Forgiveness is not an option. Death to self is a daily choice. Living is do to the will of God, the Father.

We need a fresh revelation of the cross in our lives.

Jesus was very clear that we also must choose to carry our own cross – denying ourselves and letting go of our own plans (see Matthew 10:38; 16:24).

This is good news! For the message of the cross is power to us who are being saved (see 1 Corinthians 1:17–19)!

**Contact Sword of Fire Ministries at:**

PO Box 1

Southampton

SO16 7BW

www.swordfire.org

We hope you enjoyed reading this New Wine book.
For details of other New Wine books
and a range of 2,000 titles from other
Word and Spirit publishers visit our website:
www.newwineministries.co.uk